THE REFERENCE SHELF   VOLUME 39 NUMBER 5

REPRESENTATIVE AMERICAN SPEECHES: 1966-1967

EDITED BY LESTER THONSSEN

Professor of Speech
Metropolitan State College of Colorado at Denver

THE H. W. WILSON COMPANY

NEW YORK   1967

THE REFERENCE SHELF

The books in this series contain reprints of articles, excerpts from books, and addresses on current issues and social trends in the United States and other countries. There are six separately bound numbers in each volume, all of which are generally published in the same calendar year. One number is a collection of recent speeches; each of the others is devoted to a single subject and gives background information and discussion from various points of view, concluding with a comprehensive bibliography.

Subscribers to the current volume receive the books as issued. The subscription rate is $12 ($15 foreign) for a volume of six numbers. Single numbers are $3 each.

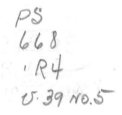

PREFACE

Like its predecessors, this volume represents a series of decisions. The speeches have been chosen from a field of several hundred. They are not necessarily the "best," for I am not sure I know what that means. But they are deserving of present notice. Hopefully, some of them may have enduring qualities. "But aren't you fearful," asked a friend of mine recently, "that certain of the choices may be unwise, and don't you wish the selections could be made by electronic wizardry that would render the decisions scientific?" To the first part of the question I give a prompt and humble Yes; to the second, a horrified No.

I am not one to urge the suppression of intellectual delights. Imagine the void created by any device that would deny readers of anthologies the high pleasure of saying, upon first opening the book, "Why, pray tell, did the compiler choose this poem or essay or speech, and not include the ones that I consider infinitely better?" Such second-guessing provides a cheerful fillip to reading. It is a joy shared by all. And it is wholesome. Who among us is so insensitive and self-effacing as not to revel in the knowledge that he could do the job more wisely?

A few months ago, I was in a party of six attending a lecture by a nationally recognized authority in his field. At the close of the speech, we assessed what we had heard. Four of us thought the speech laboriously dull; two disagreed violently. Who was right? As critics, we were, I believe, of equal competence—or incompetence, depending on what a show of hands would reveal. Doubtless the speech—if included in this or any other compilation—would get a mixed reception. Many would like it; others would question the sanity of the compiler for choosing it. The publisher might regard it as the proverbial last straw, and quietly fire the compiler. Several years ago I reprinted a speech in which I did not have limitless confidence. It was satisfactory in its area, but not distinctive. Two of my friends shared the impression, but we somehow felt that it could properly be included. To my surprise, it has been used frequently for illustrative purposes. On the other hand, certain addresses which appeared to have uncommon strength have been ignored or swiftly forgotten, to my honest surprise.

This expresses no new truth. I am repeating the obvious: One had better not expect a uniform response to a given speech, perhaps happily so. And the compiler who hopes to please all his readers is living in a dream world anchored to reality by filmy gossamer. The search for unanimous acceptance or agreement, however lofty the ideal, had better be pursued with a finely honed sense of humor. Too serious preoccupation with its attainment could result in jangled nerves and hurt sensibilities.

The compiler examines many addresses, discards most of them—sometimes for reasons obscure to himself and baffling to his readers. Doubtless the process of choice contains a mysterious element, and the nature of the mystery changes with the predispositions, prejudices, and inclinations of the compilers. In all likelihood, anthologists include many pieces just because they like them and believe their public should read them. Whether or not they should—or will—depends upon their sharing a comparable set of values and views toward man and the world.

Some years ago I referred to a criterion of selection—at the most basic level—in which I still have confidence. Is this a speech I like to listen to, or read? Any address that fails to clear this preliminary test is automatically put in a doubtful category. I am not saying it must be instantly interesting, whatever that may mean, for I share Joseph Wood Krutch's conviction that at times "something which needs very much to be learned cannot possibly be made as vivid, picturesque, dramatic and interesting as certain other things." Before me is the twenty-five-volume set of Mayo W. Hazeltine's *Orations from Homer to William McKinley,* which a friend recently located for me. As I browse through the collection, I come upon many speeches which, by our standards, are far from interesting. In fact, they are drowsily dull. Yet one can with profit and satisfaction read and reread them, for they deal with dynamic ideas that mattered in man's experience. They are, with exceptions of course, speeches that one likes to read because in them one senses the strength of men, an expansiveness of intellectual conception, and a certain grasp of a significant moment in personal or national experience.

Nothing I have said so far sheds the penetrating light of a laser beam on the question: How does one make the choices? Admittedly, in any given year, the selections are controlled largely by the supply of superior statements and the compiler's access to them. And apart from the criteria of rhetorical artistry and craftsmanship, five considerations act as partial guidelines in the selection of the speeches:

1. I believe the choice should reflect man's concern for the urgent problems of his time. Accordingly, it would be unthinkable, in my judgment, not to include one or more speeches on the Vietnamese crisis, even though a better speech, technically, on a topic of minor importance were readily available.

2. In the main, selections should deal in ideas that are persistent. Which is to say, they may be repetitious, but that is the pattern of life. The critical point is: Do the ideas make a difference in men's lives? Is the current restatement of the old theme sufficiently distinctive to warrant renewed attention?

3. New voices should be represented in successive editions. The compilation of this or any comparable work would be relatively simple if one were content to restock each issue with the established names and acknowledged masters. This is not to say that the best models should be omitted in 1966-1967 because they have appeared before. Were this the rule, the series would not have been graced so frequently by the statements of Franklin D. Roosevelt, Walter Lippmann, John F. Kennedy, J. W. Fulbright, and Adlai E. Stevenson. But, other circumstances permitting, new voices should be heard. In 1965-1966, for example, eleven of the seventeen contributors had not previously spoken through the pages of this series; in this edition, nine speakers are represented for the first time.

4. Choices are sometimes made with an eye to their pedagogical utility, with the awareness that the series is intended for a wide audience from the secondary schools through the colleges. A given

speech may be far from a model and yet present features which are
serviceable for teaching purposes.

5. Finally, I believe the reader should, if he is so disposed, be
able to learn something from each speech included in an anthology.
The content should be sufficiently substantive to provide insights of
fact and interpretation that will make a reader feel he is a better
informed person for having examined the text.

In a recent review, Penn Kimball of the Columbia Graduate
School of Journalism remarked that "an anthology of the best of
anything in any given field in any one year is not calculated to stop
a customer in his tracks." Despite unalloyed enthusiasm for his
work, a compiler can readily agree. Not all—in fact, only a frac-
tional part—of his selections will remain firmly in memory. To
hope for a better fate is unrealistic. But if a few survive the batter-
ings of time and criticism, the compiler, if still among the upright,
may take some comfort in what his advancing age will tell him was
wisdom in selection, and what his younger associates may say was
an accident of history. Reflecting on his role as a selector of poetry
for publication in *Saturday Review*, John Ciardi remarked: "And
who would not be satisfied to find that twenty years and 2,000-plus
poems later, he has managed to pick as many as fifty that seemed
to have bored their way into the memories of some of those who care
about poetry?" I will settle for a smaller number of speeches.

This edition, the thirtieth in the series, contains several speeches
that may properly be called long: not comparable in length, of
course, with the sustained orations of William Pitt, Charles James
Fox, Edmund Burke, Daniel Webster, or Edward Everett—but still
reasonably long. They are, however, important statements on ideas
fraught with significance for our time. And they underscore con-
flicting lines of thought on some of the frightening urgencies in
American society.

Skipping from these random and subjective notes on the enigma
of selection, I turn to matters on which I have no doubt. Dedicated
well-wishers and friends have again favored me with their help and
counsel. Chief among them are John Jamieson and Ruth Ulman of
The H. W. Wilson Company, Dean Keats R. McKinney of the

Metropolitan State College of Colorado, Mary Margaret Robb of the University of Colorado, Dorothea Thonssen, Marva McKinney, Ruth Taylor, Sandi Schloffman, Owen Peterson of Louisiana State University, and Dr. Ward Darley and Dr. E. Stewart Taylor of the University of Colorado Medical School at Denver.

LESTER THONSSEN

Denver, Colorado
August 1967

CONTENTS

THE ANGUISH AND THE HOPE

SPEECH AT A JOINT SESSION OF THE TENNESSEE STATE LEGISLATURE [1]

LYNDON B. JOHNSON [2]

"We shall stay the course," said President Lyndon B. Johnson in his speech before the Tennessee State Legislature on March 15, 1967. A reaffirmation of the stand steadfastly adhered to since the beginning of the Vietnam war, it voiced the American commitment to achieve the eventual peace that "will leave the people of South Vietnam free to fashion their own political and economic institutions without fear of terror or intimidation from the North."

The President's policy in Vietnam had been under severe fire, not only from activist groups in the colleges and universities, but also from men in high public office, many from his own political party. Without referring to anyone by name—though obviously the statements by Senators J. W. Fulbright, Robert F. Kennedy, Ernest Gruening, and Wayne Morse, among others, were in memory—he defended his actions with renewed confidence and firmness. To the critics who roundly condemn the continued bombing of North Vietnam, he replied that his information confirmed the judgment that the air strikes were causing "serious disruption and [were] bringing about added burdens to the North Vietnamese infiltration effort." Moreover, he asserted, the United States had on three occasions—May 1965, late December 1965 to early January 1966, and February 1967—halted bombings, hoping that Hanoi would thereby be more disposed to enter upon negotiations. But the bombing pause had been fruitless. Consistent with his repeated declaration to join Hanoi at the peace table, he announced the appointment of Ellsworth Bunker, an uncommonly skillful negotiator of wide foreign experience, to take on the job of pacification following the completion of Henry Cabot Lodge's stay in Saigon. Additionally, he spoke of the forthcoming meeting of American and South Vietnamese leaders in Guam to reassess the military action and to plan for early reconciliation.

To some observers of the political scene, the Nashville speech had a tough component, suggesting perhaps a continued escalation of the

[1] Nashville, Tennessee, March 15, 1967. Text furnished by the press secretary to the President.

[2] For biographical note, see Appendix.

war, or a drive for a "military victory." The President's tone, said James
Reston of the New York *Times,* was not boastful—rather "calmly determined, like a poker player who has made up his mind to raise the stakes."

A speculative note of possible interest to students of public address:
To what extent, if at all, does locale affect the tone of oratory? The speech
before the Tennessee Legislature coincided roughly in time with the
two hundredth anniversary of the birth of Andrew Jackson. And the
President said that coming to Tennessee was like a homecoming. There
seemed to be a special relevancy of Jacksonian courage to the decisions
which the present Administration had to make in Southeast Asia—a point
to which the President alluded in his morning talk at the Hermitage.
The Nashville address was generally characterized as a confident statement—one in which the President confronted his critics boldly and with
composed assurance. There is a feeling that Mr. Johnson is more at home
before a Southern audience than elsewhere. This prompts us to wonder
how much congeniality of atmosphere contributes to the mood and temper
of a speech. The rhetorical effect of locale, if indeed there was any,
would, however, be associated importantly with delivery, since the manu-
script was doubtless prepared at the White House.

It is always a very special privilege and pleasure for me to visit
Tennessee.

For a Texan, it is like homecoming, because much of the courage
and hard work that went into the building of the Southwest came
from the hills and the fields of Tennessee. It strengthened the sinews
of thousands of men—at the Alamo, at San Jacinto, and at the
homes of our pioneer people.

This morning, I visited the Hermitage, the historic home of Andrew Jackson. Two centuries have passed since that most American
of all Americans was born. The world has changed a great deal
since his day. But the qualities which sustain men and nations in
positions of leadership have not changed.

In our time, as in Andrew Jackson's, freedom has its price.

In our time, as in his, history conspires to test the American will.

In our time, as in Jackson's time, courage and vision, and the
willingness to sacrifice, will sustain the cause of freedom.

This generation of Americans is making its imprint on history.
It is making it in the fierce hills and the sweltering jungles of Vietnam. I think most of our citizens—after a very penetrating debate

which is our democratic heritage—have reached a common understanding on the meaning and on the objectives of that struggle.

Before I discuss the specific questions that remain at issue, I should like to review the points of widespread agreement.

It was two years ago that we were forced to choose, forced to make a decision between major commitments in defense of South Vietnam or retreat—the evacuation of more than 25,000 of our troops, the collapse of the Republic of Vietnam in the face of subversion and external assault.

Andrew Jackson would never have been surprised at the choice we made.

We chose a course in keeping with American tradition, in keeping with the foreign policy of at least three administrations, with the expressed will of the Congress of the United States, with our solemn obligations under the Southeast Asian Treaty, and with the interest of 16 million South Vietnamese who had no wish to live under Communist domination.

As our commitment in Vietnam required more men and more equipment, some voices were raised in opposition. The Administration was urged to disengage, to find an excuse to abandon the effort.

These cries came despite growing evidence that the defense of Vietnam held the key to the political and economic future of free Asia. The stakes of the struggle grew correspondingly.

It became clear that if we were prepared to stay the course in Vietnam, we could help to lay the cornerstone for a diverse and independent Asia, full of promise and resolute in the cause of peaceful economic development for her long-suffering peoples.

But if we faltered, the forces of chaos would scent victory and decades of strife and aggression would stretch endlessly before us.

The choice was clear. We would stay the course. We shall stay the course.

I think most Americans support this fundamental decision. Most of us remember the fearful cost of ignoring aggression. Most of us have cast aside the illusion that we can live in an affluent fortress while the world slides into chaos.

I think we have all reached broad agreement on our basic objectives in Vietnam.

First, an honorable peace, that will leave the people of South Vietnam free to fashion their own political and economic institutions without fear of terror or intimidation from the North.

Second, a Southeast Asia in which all countries—including a peaceful North Vietnam—apply their scarce resources to the real problems of their people: combating hunger, ignorance, and diseases.

I have said many, many times, that nothing would give us greater pleasure than to invest our own resources in the constructive works of peace rather than in the futile destruction of war.

Third, a concrete demonstration that aggression across international frontiers or demarcation lines is no longer an acceptable means of political change.

There is, I think, a general agreement among Americans on the things that we do not want in Vietnam.

We do not want permanent bases. We will begin with the withdrawal of our troops on a reasonable schedule whenever reciprocal concessions are forthcoming from our adversary.

We do not seek to impose our political beliefs upon South Vietnam. Our republic rests upon a brisk commerce in ideas. We will be happy to see free competition in the intellectual marketplace whenever North Vietnam is willing to shift the conflict from the battlefield to the ballot box.

So, these are the broad principles on which most Americans agree.

On a less general level, however, the events and frustrations of these past few difficult weeks have inspired a number of questions about our Vietnam policy in the minds and hearts of a good many of our citizens. Today, here in this historical chamber, I want to deal with some of those questions that figure most prominently in the press and in some of the letters which reach a President's desk.

Many Americans are confused by the barrage of information about military engagements. They long for the capsule summary which has kept tabs on our previous wars, a line on the map that divides friend from foe.

Precisely what, they ask, is our military situation, and what are the prospects of victory?

The first answer is that Vietnam is aggression in a new guise, as far removed from trench warfare as the rifle from the longbow. This is a war of infiltration, of subversion, of ambush. Pitched battles are very rare, and even more rarely are they decisive.

Today, more than 1 million men from the Republic of Vietnam and its six allies are engaged in the order of battle.

Despite continuing increases in North Vietnam infiltration, this strengthening of allied forces in 1966 under the brilliant leadership of General Westmoreland, was instrumental in reversing the whole course of this war.

We estimate that 55,000 North Vietnamese and Vietcong were killed in 1966, compared with 35,000 the previous year. More were wounded, and more than 20,000 defected.

By contrast, 9,500 South Vietnamese, more than 5,000 Americans, and 600 from other allied forces were killed in action.

The Vietnamese Army achieved a 1966 average of two weapons captured from the Vietcong to every one lost, a dramatic turnaround from the previous two years.

Allied forces have made several successful sweeps through territories that were formerly considered Vietcong sanctuaries only a short time ago. These operations not only cost the enemy large numbers of men and weapons, but are very damaging to his morale.

What does all of this mean? Will the North Vietnamese change their tactics? Will there be less infiltration of main units? Will there be more of guerilla warfare?

The actual truth is we just don't know.

What we do know is that General Westmoreland's strategy is producing results, that our military situation has substantially improved, that our military success has permitted the groundwork to be laid for a pacification program which is the long-run key to an independent South Vietnam.

Since February, 1965, our military operations have included selective bombing of military targets in North Vietnam. Our purposes are three:

To back our fighting men by denying the enemy a sanctuary;

To exact a penalty against North Vietnam for her flagrant violations of the Geneva Accords of 1954 and 1962;

To limit the flow, or to substantially increase the cost of infiltration of men and matériel from North Vietnam.

Our intelligence confirms that we have been successful.

Yet, some of our people object strongly to this aspect of our policy. Must we bomb, many people will ask. Does it do any military good? Is it consistent with America's limited objectives? Is it an inhuman act that is aimed at civilians?

On the question of military utility, I can only report the firm belief of the Secretary of Defense, the Joint Chiefs of Staff, the Central Intelligence Agency, General Westmoreland and our commanders in the field, and all the sources of information and advice available to the Commander-in-Chief and that is that the bombing is causing serious disruption and is bringing about added burdens to the North Vietnamese infiltration effort.

We know, for example, that half a million people are kept busy just repairing damage to bridges, roads, railroads, and other strategic facilities, and in air and coastal defense and repair of power plants.

I also want to say categorically that it is not the position of the American Government that the bombing will be decisive in getting Hanoi to abandon aggression. It has, however, created very serious problems for them. The best indication of how substantial is the fact that they are working so hard every day with all their friends throughout the world to try to get us to stop.

The bombing is entirely consistent with America's limited objectives in South Vietnam. The strength of Communist main-force units in the South is clearly based on their infiltration from the North. I think it is simply unfair to our American soldiers, sailors, and marines and our Vietnamese allies to ask them to face increased enemy personnel and fire power without making an effort to try to reduce that infiltration.

As to bombing civilians, I would simply say that we are making an effort that is unprecedented in the history of warfare to be sure that we do not. It is our policy to bomb military targets only.

We have never deliberately bombed cities, nor attacked any target with the purpose of inflicting civilian casualties.

We hasten to add, however, that we recognize, and we regret, that some people, even after warning, are living and working in the vicinity of military targets and they have suffered.

We are also too aware that men and machines are not infallible, and that some mistakes do occur.

But our record on this account is, in my opinion, highly defensible.

Look for a moment at the record of the other side.

Any civilian casualties that result from our operations are inadvertent, in stark contrast to the calculated Vietcong policy of systematic terror.

Tens of thousands of innocent Vietnamese civilians have been killed, tortured, and kidnapped by the Vietcong. There is no doubt about the deliberate nature of the Vietcong program. One need only note the frequency with which Vietcong victims are village leaders, teachers, health workers, and others who are trying to carry out constructive programs for their people.

Yet, the deeds of the Vietcong go largely unnoted in the public debate. It is this moral double bookkeeping which makes us get sometimes very weary of our critics.

But there is another question that we should answer: Why don't we stop bombing to make it easier to begin negotiations?

The answer is a simple one:

We stopped for five days and twenty hours in May 1965. Representatives of Hanoi simply returned our message in a plain envelope.

We stopped bombing for thirty-six days and fifteen hours in December 1965 and January 1966. Hanoi only replied: "A political settlement of the Vietnam problem can be envisaged only when the United States Government has accepted the four-point stand of the Government of the Democratic Republic of Vietnam, has proved this by actual deeds, has stopped unconditionally and for good its air raids and all other acts of war against the Democratic Republic of Vietnam."

Only last month we stopped bombing for five days and eighteen hours, after many prior weeks in which we had communicated to them several possible routes to peace, any one of which America was prepared to take. Their response, as you know, delivered to His Holiness the Pope, was this: The United States "must put an end to their aggression in Vietnam, end unconditionally and definitively the bombing and all other acts of war against the Democratic Republic of Vietnam, withdraw from South Vietnam all American and satellite troops, recognize the South Vietnamese National Front for Liberation, and let the Vietnamese people settle themselves their own affairs."

That is where we stand today.

They have three times rejected a bombing pause as a means to open the way to ending the war, and go together to the negotiating table.

The tragedy of South Vietnam is not limited to casualty lists.

There is much tragedy in the story of a nation at war for nearly a generation. It is the story of economic stagnation. It is the story of a generation of young men—the flower of the labor force—pressed into military service by one side or the other.

No one denies that the survival of South Vietnam is heavily dependent upon early economic progress.

My most recent and my most hopeful report of progress in this area came from an old friend of Tennessee, of the Tennessee Valley Authority—David Lilienthal, who recently went as my representative to Vietnam to begin to work with the Vietnamese people on economic planning for that area.

He reported—and with some surprise, I might add—that he discovered an extraordinary air of confidence among the farmers, village leaders, trade unionists, and the industrialists. He concluded that their economic behavior suggests "that they think they know how all of this is going to come out."

Mr. Lilienthal also said that the South Vietnamese were among the hardest working people that he had seen in developing countries around the world, that "to have been through twenty years of war and still have this amount of 'zip' almost ensures their long-term economic development."

Mr. Lilienthal will be going with me to Guam Saturday night to talk with our new leaders about the plans he will try to institute there.

Our AID programs are supporting the drive toward this sound economy.

But none of these economic accomplishments will be decisive by itself. And no economic achievement can substitute for a strong and free political structure.

We cannot build such a structure—because only the Vietnamese can do that.

I think they are building it. As I am talking to you here, a freely elected constituent assembly in Saigon is now wrestling with the last details of a new constitution, one which will bring the Republic of Vietnam to full membership among the democratic nations of the world.

We expect that constitution to be completed this month.

In the midst of war, they have been building for peace and justice. That is a remarkable accomplishment in the annals of mankind.

Ambassador Henry Cabot Lodge, who has served us with such great distinction, is coming to the end of his second distinguished tour of duty in Saigon.

To replace him, I am drafting as our Ambassador to the Government of Vietnam, Mr. Ellsworth Bunker—able and devoted, full of wisdom and experience acquired on five continents over many years.

As his Deputy, I am nominating and recalling from Pakistan, Mr. Eugene Locke, our young and very vigorous Ambassador to Pakistan.

To drive forward with a sense of urgency the work in pacification in Vietnam, I am sending Presidential Assistant Robert Komer.

To strengthen General Westmoreland in the intensive operations that he will be conducting in the months ahead, I am assigning to him additional top-flight military personnel, the best that the country has been able to provide.

So you can be confident that in the months ahead we shall have at work in Saigon the ablest, the wisest, the most tenacious, and the most experienced team that the United States of America can mount.

In view of these decisions and in view of the meetings that will take place this weekend, I thought it wise to invite the leaders of South Vietnam to join us in Guam for a part of our discussions, if it were convenient for them. I am gratified to be informed that they have accepted our invitation.

I should also like for you to know that the representatives of all the countries that are contributing troops in Vietnam will be coming to Washington for April 20 and 21 meetings for a general appraisal of the situation that exists.

This brings me to my final point, the peaceful and just world that we all seek.

We have just lived through another flurry of rumors of "peace feelers."

Our years of dealing with this problem have taught us that peace will not come easily.

The problem is a very simple one: it takes two to negotiate at a peace table and Hanoi has just simply refused to consider coming to a peace table.

I don't believe that our own position on peace negotiations can be stated any more clearly than I have stated it many times in the past—or that the distinguished Secretary of State, Mr. Rusk, or Ambassador Goldberg, or any number of other officials have stated it in every forum that we could find.

I do want to repeat to you this afternoon—and through you to the people of America—the essentials now, lest there be any doubts.

United States representatives are ready at any time for discussions of the Vietnam problem or any related matter, with any government or governments, if there is any reason to believe that these discussions will in any way seriously advance the cause of peace.

We are prepared to go more than halfway and to use any avenue possible to encourage such discussions. And we have done that at every opportunity.

We believe that the Geneva Accords of 1954 and 1962 could serve as the central elements of a peaceful settlement. These accords provide, in essence, that both South and North Vietnam should be free from external interference, while at the same time they would be free independently to determine their positions on the question of reunification.

We also stand ready to advance toward a reduction of hostilities, without prior agreement. The road to peace could go from deeds to discussions, or it could start with discussions and go to deeds.

We are ready to take either route. We are ready to move on both of them.

Reciprocity must be the fundamental principle of any reduction in hostilities. The United States cannot and will not reduce its activities unless and until there is some reduction on the other side. To follow any other rule would be to violate the trust that we undertake when we ask a man to risk his life for his country.

We will negotiate a reduction of the bombing whenever the Government of North Vietnam is ready and there are almost innumerable avenues of communication by which the Government of North Vietnam can make their readiness known.

To this date and this hour, there has been no sign of that readiness.

Yet, we must—and we will—keep trying.

As I speak to you today, Secretary Rusk and our representatives throughout the world are on a constant alert. Hundreds and hundreds of quiet diplomatic conversations, free from the glare of front-page headlines, or of klieg lights, are being held and they will be held on the possibilities of bringing peace to Vietnam.

Governor Averell Harriman, with twenty-five years of experience of troubleshooting on the most difficult international problems that America has ever had, is carrying out my instructions that every possible lead, however slight it may first appear, from any source, public or private, shall be followed up.

Let me conclude by saying this: I so much wish that it were within my power to assure that all those in Hanoi could hear one simple message—America is committed to the defense of South Vietnam until an honorable peace can be negotiated.

If this one communication gets through and its rational implications are drawn, we should be at the table tomorrow. It would be none too soon for us. Then hundreds of thousands of Americans— as brave as any who ever took the field for their country—could come back home.

And the man who could lead them back is the man whom you trained and sent from here, our own beloved, brilliant General "Westy" Westmoreland. As these heroes came back to their homes, millions of Vietnamese could begin to make a decent life for themselves and their families without fear of terrorism, without fear of war, or without fear of Communist enslavement.

That is what we are working and fighting for. We must not—we shall not—and we will not—fail.

REPORT ON VIETNAM AND EAST ASIA [3]

EDWARD W. BROOKE [4]

Teachers of argumentation often remind their students and themselves of the necessity and propriety of withholding judgment until the evidence has been examined and of facing up to a change of conviction if the data on the opposing side are sufficiently compelling to require it. Just how seriously the majority of mankind takes this advice is arguable. Our built-in rationalizations often spare us the pain of following it. But in many cases, happily, we do change our minds, and it is always revealing to analyze the reasons for the shift. Over the years, the editor has from time to time assigned projects in which selected students were invited to speak about a change of view which they had experienced on a matter of some consequence. Two such talks delivered years ago remain indelibly fixed: one in which a young man gave a poignantly insightful analysis of his shift from opposition to endorsement of compulsory military service; the other, of a change of belief regarding the Communist ideology. But, by and large, this is a difficult kind of speechmaking, in class or out, and when a good specimen comes along, proper note should be made of it. Herewith that acknowledgment.

On March 23, 1967, Senator Edward W. Brooke, Republican of Massachusetts, delivered a detailed report before the United States Senate on his recent visit to Southeast Asia. Prior to taking the tour, he had been, as he observed, "critical of the President's foreign policy, and critical of his conduct of the war." During the past year he had argued "that the United States . . . ought to take the first step toward creating a better climate for negotiations"; and he had "long debated whether to recommend either a pause in the bombing of North Vietnam or some other military de-escalation which might . . . persuade Hanoi to enter serious negotiations." In a distinctively temperate, clear, and forthright summary of the facts and impressions gathered from his visit, he concluded—reluctantly, he admitted—that "the enemy is not disposed to participate in meaningful negotiations at this time" and that "the general direction of our present military efforts in Vietnam is necessary."

It takes courage to make such a speech, for the repercussions can easily be anticipated. Any announcement of a shift in position, especially on the critical matter of war and peace, is certain to provoke some angry replies. He got a good many. But the echoes of praise resounded more

[3] United States Senate, March 23, 1967. Text furnished by Senator Brooke, with permission for this reprint.

[4] For biographical note, see Appendix.

distinctly. Senator Thomas H. Kuchel of California, commending the "clarity of thought" and "force of his logic," said Mr. Brooke's speech was "a highly constructive contribution to a tragically complex American and world problem." Reporter Roscoe Drummond said of Senator Brooke: "He is the right man saying the right thing at the right time." Observing that others had said substantially the same things on the war, Drummond attributed the special impact of the address to "the manner of the man himself." "Senator Brooke shows that he has the courage, capacity, and willingness to change his mind—not because he was pressured by others, but because his own honest thinking required him to do so."

Senator Brooke's speech makes another claim on our attention. It is a maiden speech. The former Attorney General of Massachusetts took his seat in the United States Senate in January 1967. Since then he has been much sought after for speaking engagements (reportedly receiving some fourteen hundred invitations in a little over two months). But not until March 23 did he take the floor to make a major statement.

Maiden speeches are traditionally regarded as difficult experiences. They must satisfy the high expectations that the listening and reading public, of all political persuasions, ordinarily sets. So William Pitt and Richard Brinsley Sheridan found out, the former with high success, the latter with considerably less. While the contemporary orator in his maiden venture does not usually encounter the incivility that was fairly common in British parliamentary speaking, he must still show high proficiency to avoid criticism. The combination of a maiden speech and a change of view makes the test doubly severe. Senator Brooke met the challenge with noteworthy power.

In 1967 Senator Brooke received the Delta Sigma Rho-Tau Kappa Alpha Speaker of the Year Award.

Mr. President, when I stood for election to the seat in the United States Senate from Massachusetts which was being vacated by my distinguished predecessor, Leverett Saltonstall, the opposition party, in the true spirit of partisan politics, advised the Massachusetts electorate not to vote for me because I was critical of the Administration's foreign policy, and in particular, of the Administration's conduct of the war in Vietnam. The Massachusetts voters were further advised to elect my opponent, for he would give 100 per cent backing to the Administration in its conduct of the war. I understand this as in the nature of American politics. For naturally, the Democratic party wished to elect a second Senator from Massachusetts. Very candidly, I am sure the Republican party would have followed a similar course under similar circumstances.

I advised the people of Massachusetts that if they wanted the executive and legislative branches of Government to be one and the same, and if they wanted a United States Senator to be, in effect, a rubber stamp for the President, then they should elect my opponent. But, on the other hand, if they wanted the executive and legislative branches to be checks upon one another, and if they wanted independent judgment in the United States Senate, then I ask them to support my candidacy. I am pleased to report, this they did.

On one point, the opposition was right: I was critical of the President's foreign policy, and critical of his conduct of the war. But I was never critical in a partisan manner.

My purpose was only to seek alternatives and solutions to the particularly grave problems which were confronting the American people and the peoples of the world.

Upon taking my seat in this great deliberative body, I immediately began to ask questions of the senior Members of the Senate and the House, the Departments of State and Defense, intellectuals, writers, and learned members of the press. I read, and advised my staff to read, everything possible about Vietnam and Southeast Asia. For I considered—as I still do—Vietnam and Southeast Asia to be currently the most important issue with which our Government must concern itself.

The state which I represent has a very active and well-informed spiritual leadership and a large academic community. And perhaps more than most states, it has sharp, defined, and knowledgeable opinions about Vietnam. My mail, phone calls, and personal visits by constituents on this subject have been voluminous. Like most Americans, I was hopeful that the Tet truce would be extended and would lead to negotiations for peace. But when the bombing in North Vietnam was resumed, I felt that I could no longer sit in the Senate, so far away from Vietnam, and make intelligent decisions without getting first-hand knowledge of the situation.

For when I was a boy, my father told me that the quality of a man's judgment was no better than the quality of his information. It was in this spirit that I asked my distinguished colleagues, Senator John Sparkman and Senator Wallace Bennett, chairman and ranking minority member of the Banking and Currency Committee, of which I am a member, for approval to go to Vietnam and other east Asian countries in order to study the economies of those nations, the effects of our enormous spending on those economies, and the political and military situations there.

I must confess that I did entertain preconceived ideals and opinions concerning the war. Nevertheless, I believe that I went to Southeast Asia with an open mind and with all of the objectivity that I could muster.

For whatever value my findings, impressions, conclusions, and recommendations may have to my colleagues in the Senate and the House, to the executive branch of our Government, and to the American and Southeast Asian peoples, I respectfully submit them.

In my search for knowledge, I visited Japan, Taiwan, Hong Kong, South Vietnam, Cambodia, and Thailand. In each place, I conferred with government officials and with a variety of private citizens. I spoke with soldiers and with intellectuals, with politicians and with farmers. I took full advantage of the wisdom and experience offered by the competent men and women whom I found in the Foreign Service of the United States. I spent as much time as possible seeing at first hand examples of those things which had been discussed in briefings, asking questions, and testing fundamental American policies against the harsh light of the realities of a distant and far different continent.

I first went to Japan, which is undoubtedly the grandest success story in all of Asia. I allotted only a brief portion of my trip to Japan and will refer to it simply in passing today.

Less than a generation after the conclusion of a disastrous war, Japan has made a remarkable recovery. It enjoys a stable democracy and a flourishing economy. It has adopted much that is good in Western civilization while holding on to its own traditional values and culture. And this is good, for diversity is good. We do not want a world where all people look alike, dress alike, talk alike, and even worse, think alike. The strength of the world will come not from sameness, but from magnificent pluralism.

The soundness of American postwar policy in Japan should be recognized. But most of the credit must go to the genius, the industry, and the spirit of the Japanese people themselves. For they were determined to create a viable society out of ashes and to construct new political, social, and economic foundations to replace the military and imperialist regimes of the 1930's and 1940's. They have obviously learned that the road to world prestige and higher standards of living for their people is the road of economic and social progress, and not the road of geographic expansionism.

To travel from Japan to Taiwan is to travel from an already developed, highly sophisticated nation to one that is well on the way to similar economic and social well-being. Taiwan is literally moving from a bicycle economy through a motorcycle economy and into an automobile economy.

In Taiwan, I consulted with, among others, the Vice President and Prime Minister, Mr. C. K. Yen; the Economic Minister, Mr. K. T. Li; and the Vice Minister for Foreign Affairs, Mr. H. K. Yang. As elsewhere, I also talked with private citizens, including the Governor of the Central Bank of China, Mr. Kan Lee, and the President of the China Development Corporation, Mr. Felix Chang. In addition, I visited the Legislative Yuan, as well as a variety of industrial and agricultural projects, and academic institutions. I was most favorably impressed with the quality and dedication of the political and business leadership in Taiwan.

The economic progress which has been made by this island nation is truly remarkable. Its progress has been accomplished in the face of severe handicaps. An unusually large percentage of able-bodied men, who normally would be productive members of the economy, are diverted into the Nationalist Chinese military, which now numbers some 600,000 of a population of approximately 13 million. Furthermore, Taiwan has a surprisingly youthful population. Fifty per cent of its people are fifteen years of age or under. And yet, the gross national product of Taiwan for 1966 was an exceptional $3 billion. With the exception of Public Law 480—the food for peace program—formal United States aid programs have been eliminated. The country is also turning more toward private enterprise principles as the government divests itself of much of its property holdings. As a result, Taiwan continues to attract substantial amounts of private foreign capital which serve to replace the assistance formerly provided by the United States Government. Great strides have also been made in compulsory education, public health, and living standards. And this progress will undoubtedly be continued.

In addition, Taiwan has begun to play a constructive role in international affairs. It has already initiated a very successful African aid program, based upon some of the principles of our own AID plan. I believe that we may be justifiably proud of our assistance programs in Taiwan, and of the people who have administered them.

It is evident that the entire psychological and philosophical foundation of the Nationalist Chinese government is the desire and intention to return to the mainland. This has resulted in a grossly disproportionate governmental structure, which has been developed and maintained for the purpose of administering all of mainland China rather than of meeting the more limited requirements imposed by the problems of Taiwan.

Nevertheless, United States policy with respect to Taiwan must not be colored by the fear of the Nationalist Chinese insistence that they will one day return to their homeland. We must observe more closely what is done on Taiwan, and concern ourselves less with fears engendered by what is said. Unless dramatic reversals occur— and I found no such symptoms—the Republic of China, will continue to develop, to feed, to clothe, and to house its people. It will also continue to play a more significant and cooperative role in international affairs. As a nation committed to the ideals of democracy and to free enterprise, as a stanch ally of the United States, and as a successful recipient of an intelligent United States program of economic assistance, the Republic of China stands as a symbol of what our foreign political and economic policies can and should accomplish.

I next went to Hong Kong, a British crown colony with a population of 3,750,000, of which over 98 per cent are Chinese. Hong

Kong's business community, finance, port, and related facilities are very highly developed, and unusual wealth and affluence can be found within its total 397.75-square-mile area. Unfortunately, there is also dire poverty in Hong Kong, the likes of which I personally have never witnessed in the worst part of the United States or anywhere else in the world. Sampans mired in the mud and housing four, six, or eight persons, and filth and disease surpassing description are found within five hundred yards of beautiful homes owned by successful businessmen. Within a mile of the colony's impressive business center are hillsides containing ramshackle huts housing thousands of Chinese refugees. Although the government of the colony has made progress in refugee relocation by the development of public refugee housing centers, several of which I visited, the major problems posed by the refugee influx must still be resolved. In the course of my stay, I spoke with several officials, in addition to representatives of private organizations, including Roman Catholic and Lutheran missions. I will expand upon my findings and conclusions with respect to the colony's economic situation in my report to the Committee on Banking and Currency.

But, very frankly, my primary purpose in going to Hong Kong was to talk with as many "China watchers" as possible, in order to get information concerning economic, political, social, and military problems on the mainland. These China watchers gather their information from Chinese radio broadcasts, Chinese newspapers, Chinese refugees from the mainland, and from Chinese living in Hong Kong who correspond and visit with relatives and friends on the mainland. Recently, much information has also come from "wall posters," an institution which is somewhat familiar in the Orient and at times surprisingly accurate. In addition, much knowledge is gained from the wisdom of Chinese citizens who reside in Hong Kong and from their frequently informed, sometimes intuitive, sense of what is transpiring within China's closed society.

Mainland China is of such tremendous concern to the United States, and the problems posed by its existence and possible direction are so complex, that no easy approach or solution is possible.

No reasonable man would attempt to resolve the many problems of United States policy toward Communist China on the basis of a brief visit to east Asia, or insist that the present situation could not change radically and without warning in a short period of time. However, my trip has enabled me to arrive at some tentative conclusions with respect to at least the immediate future of Communist China which I feel should be shared with my colleagues in the Senate and with the American people.

My basic conclusion is that Peking's threat to the rest of Asia—at least for the foreseeable future—has been overestimated. The history of China under Mao Tse-tung has been one concerned predominantly with internal affairs. Mao Tse-tung appears to have concentrated, for the most part, upon the development of his own form of a Communist society within the borders of mainland China. He has been concerned with the country's economic development, and—despite the failure of the "Great Leap Forward" begun in 1958—has managed to improve in some areas upon the mistakes made by the old Nationalist regime.

Mao Tse-tung's obsession with the form of society in his own country has been made even more apparent by the recent "cultural revolution." Concerned that the country had wandered from the Maoist objectives of giant communes, complete elimination of private property, and the wholesale government control of production and distribution, Mao Tse-tung is taking steps to rid the Chinese Communist party of those members who appear to be less than vigorous in pursuit of his goals. But the establishment that Mao Tse-tung himself had constructed could not be altered so easily, and his attempt to remake the Chinese Communist party has resulted in violence and bloodshed. Even Mao's most trusted ally, the Red army, has been divided on questions raised by the cultural revolution. This has resulted in great divisions in the power structure and consequently in the apparent political fragmentation of the country.

For the time being, the consensus appears to be that the "cultural revolution" is waning. Although the influence of Mao's policies has perhaps waned, too, there can be little doubt that he is still held in such esteem by the overwhelming majority of party members that it would be impossible for his opponents to defeat or replace him now.

I cannot, of course, say that Peking has not been—and will not be—concerned with events in the rest of Asia, or indeed in the remainder of the world. But for the time being, I do believe that such concerns will take the form primarily of responses to the actions of other nations, particularly the United States and the Soviet Union. There is support for this belief in recent history. When the Chinese went into the Korean conflict, it was with the purpose in mind not of reestablishing Chinese domination over a neighboring Asian country, but of preventing the elimination of a Communist government in North Korea and the extension of a non-Communist power to the borders of China itself. What many people in the West considered to be an outrageously aggressive gesture may well have been viewed by the Chinese Communists as a defensive step or a form of preventive war.

The brief Chinese struggles with India have arisen over border disputes for which the Chinese claim the Indians were at least in part responsible. Without attempting to decide the merits of the controversy, it is not surprising that a nation would use military force to establish control over territory it regards as its own. Attacks by the Red Chinese upon offshore islands presently controlled by Taiwan represent an attempt by the Peking government to bring under its control areas which Peking undoubtedly considers to be historically a part of the mainland. Even though the Communist Chinese have repeatedly voiced claims to these offshore islands and certain Sino-Indian border areas, these claims have not led them to major aggression in Asia so far.

It is not my purpose to defend Communist China, but I do believe it is essential to the formulation of practical American foreign policy that we recognize the degree of restraint which China has exercised in Asia thus far. Recent history has revealed striking contrasts between Communist China's militant words and its cautious behavior.

We must estimate the degree of direct Chinese combat participation in the war in Vietnam in view of this same factor of Peking's
demonstrated reluctance to act as vehemently as she speaks. If our
military operations are escalated to the point where the mainland
Chinese consider that their own territory is threatened, we can
probably expect Chinese participation in the war. If, on the other
hand, we continue to act with restraint, making it clear to the
Chinese that we will do all in our power to limit the struggle to
Vietnam, I believe that the commitment of Chinese combat troops
in the Vietnam war is highly improbable.

I should not be misunderstood on the question of China's desire
for influence over east Asia. I do believe that China wants an end to
American presence in Asia, just as we would undoubtedly want an
end to similar Chinese or Russian presence in the Western Hemisphere. I further believe that China will support any revolution
which develops indigenously in the rest of Asia. Already, this can
be seen in such places as Vietnam, where the Chinese supply equipment to the North Vietnamese and the Vietcong, and in Thailand,
where the Chinese supply political indoctrination for the insurgents
operating in the northeast section of that country. The Chinese will
certainly try to incite revolution wherever they can, but at the
moment, at least, their policy does not appear to be one of geographic expansion.

Our policy in this area should be based upon these facts and
realities, and not upon conceptions of imperialist expansion which
grew out of our experience in Europe and in the Pacific during
World War II.

I favor maintaining our present policy with respect to recognition of Communist China and its admission to the United Nations.
The Chinese government still chooses to remain aloof from the
community of nations. I am convinced that Chinese participation
in the United Nations would not be profitable, and that China has
attached unacceptable conditions to such participation. However,
we must be sensitive to all prospects for future contact. Almost 800
million people dwell within the borders of mainland China. Their
existence cannot be ignored, and we must consistently emphasize

our earnest desire for improved relations with their government. If future Chinese leadership indicates that it is ready to take a more positive place in the world community, the United States must be ready and prepared to listen.

We must not accept the proposition that war with Communist China is inevitable, and we must do all within reason and honor to avoid such a disastrous war.

Seldom in our history has this nation been so divided on a question of foreign policy as it is with respect to our participation in the war in Vietnam. Accordingly, I devoted most of my time to this country, and to its immense problems. I talked with South Vietnamese officials, including Prime Minister Nguyen Cao Ky and Foreign Minister Tran Van Do. I conferred with Ambassador Henry Cabot Lodge and with General William C. Westmoreland and the general staff. I attended a session of the Constituent Assembly, and was present when South Vietnam's new constitution was finally adopted. I met with Donald McDonald, Director of United States AID, and with Wade Lathram, Director of OCO, and with members of their staffs, and viewed AID facilities and projects controlled by the related Office of Civilian Operations. I talked with knowledgeable members of the international press corps in Saigon. I spent much of my time outside of Saigon, traveling by helicopter to a number of military installations and to a variety of civilian projects. I viewed refugee resettlement projects, and visited a prisoner-of-war camp, where I was able to converse with captured Vietcong and North Vietnamese soldiers. I studied the so-called "Chieu Hoi"—open arms—program, designed to induce defection from the Vietcong and the North Vietnamese regular army, and I conversed with some of the Vietcong and North Vietnamese defectors at a Chieu Hoi camp. In the evenings, I made it a point to confer with many South Vietnamese citizens, representing all viewpoints. I concentrated especially upon the intellectual community, since that segment of society is not only the most likely to be well informed, but is also the most likely to be critical of governmental policy.

In one sense, I returned from Vietnam with certain beliefs unchanged. We are involved in a situation of great complexity that challenges the traditional American demand for prompt and clear-cut solutions. I have stated before that little could be gained by incessant questioning of whether our presence in Vietnam is justified. Resolution of such a question may well be important as a basis for future action. But it is academic in a context of present attempts to resolve our unhappy dilemma. It is an inescapable fact that we are in Vietnam, that we have committed a massive military and civilian presence to that country, and that we must work for a solution which will be best for South Vietnam, and most honorable and decent for ourselves.

All too frequently, the United States is subjected to the criticism that it is insensitive in its attitude toward other countries and peoples and in its conduct of foreign affairs. I believe that our present efforts in South Vietnam are the best possible defense against this charge. We may have made many mistakes in Vietnam in the past. But we are correcting them. Every effort is being made to insure that the American presence in the country will not be an overbearing or an insulting one. Virtually all of our civilian personnel are restricted to advisory positions. Ultimate decisions, and the responsibility for those decisions, belong to the South Vietnamese. Pains are taken to give prominence to South Vietnamese officials, rather than American officials, at joint functions and at ceremonies. Neither soldiers nor American civilians are allowed to enter Dalat, a lovely city which many Vietnamese people enjoy visiting. As much as possible, military personnel are kept out of the capital city of Saigon. Credit for such understanding and sensitivity must be given to the distinguished Ambassador Henry Cabot Lodge, who has established and implemented policies designed to minimize the inevitable abrasive side effects of a military presence.

The policies are working. I fought as an infantryman in the European theater during the Second World War. And despite the obvious value and necessity of American participation on behalf of our European Allies during that struggle, I well remember the substantial amount of anti-American feeling generated by our presence in Europe. I found that anti-American feeling is conspicuously absent in South Vietnam. I am convinced that the people of that country are well aware of what American presence there has meant. They believe in the main that our military assistance kept South Vietnam from succumbing to a Communist takeover in 1965. They believe that our civilian advisers have helped their country to make political, social, and economic progress which would have been impossible for South Vietnam to accomplish alone. The value of our assistance has been demonstrated. It is welcomed and appreciated by the people of South Vietnam.

Mr. President, I do not mean that the American civilian operation in South Vietnam is an unqualified success. Of course, any undertaking of this magnitude has serious problems, and this undertaking is no exception. I will expand upon some of these problems in my written report to the Banking and Currency Committee. However, at this time I want to mention a major problem, the AID administration of the port at Saigon.

Mr. President, I walked that port, I flew over it by helicopter, and I talked with seamen on barges and ships, and rode in a Navy patrol boat up the Saigon River.

The problem is one of seemingly unresolvable congestion. Commodities—sometimes perishable ones—do remain unloaded in ships and barges docked in the port for weeks and sometimes for months. Poorly planned shipping schedules contribute to this, as does the fluctuating Saigon market. Goods ordered when prices are high may not arrive until such prices have fallen considerably. In such an event, consignees often prefer to leave the cargo in port rather than claim it and suffer a loss caused by low prices.

Although AID officials have helped the South Vietnamese make some progress in relieving congestion, more must be done and at a faster pace. There must be far more orderly spacing of cargo arrivals. Consignees who refuse to claim cargoes when they arrive should be denied import licenses. And efforts should be made to convince consignees not to limit themselves to the normal eight-hour working day when claiming their goods. Observers appear to be convinced that some progress has been made but greater efforts must be made to insure that the crucial commercial import program is not defeated because of mechanical problems of port administration which can be corrected. However, it should be remembered that the Port of Saigon was constructed to handle 150,000 tons of cargo per month. The fact is that it is presently handling 300,000 tons per month, and it is expected that by the end of this year it will be handling 500,000 tons per month.

So much has been said and written about Vietnam, often by people overcome by the great emotions which the war arouses in us all, that many fundamental considerations tend to get lost or confused in public discussion. For this reason, we need constantly to remind ourselves and our adversaries of the essential elements in the American commitment to defend South Vietnam.

The President has often characterized that commitment: We are in South Vietnam to help the people of that country protect themselves against a complex form of aggression and to help them establish a political system reflecting their own desires and needs, not one conceived and imposed by external force. The very nature of this mission dictates that our military action be limited in form and in purpose.

To say that the people of South Vietnam are the stakes in this conflict is a brutal truth. But we must make clear that they are the highest stakes and not merely pawns in some larger contest. Once we depart from this principle and begin to rationalize the struggle in Vietnam as a necessary sacrifice to the global balance of power, I believe that we cross the line between a just and an unjust war. While we may recognize the wider implications of the war, we can never justify the conflict on those grounds. In my judgment, it would be plainly immoral to expect the South Vietnamese to suffer today's violence in order to ward off tomorrow's war somewhere else.

This point is elementary but highly significant for United States policy. From the beginning of United States involvement, the South Vietnamese people have had totally inadequate institutions through which to question or confirm the direction of the war. Nothing has been more imperative or more encouraging than the recent progress toward creation of such institutions. The early establishment of a more broadly based civilian government in South Vietnam will provide, for the first time, a reasonable confidence that decisions regarding the war effort will reflect popular interests and aspirations. This will help insure that local issues, and not the sweeping complications of international politics, govern allied action.

I also believe that the process launched by the new constitution for South Vietnam provides the most effective pressure for political settlement of the war. The new government will have an opportunity to make a fresh start toward national reconciliation with those South Vietnamese now collaborating with Hanoi and the National Liberation Front. The move toward constitutional government also confronts the Vietcong with an urgent need to reassess their political goals. Previously, they have followed a doctrine of rule or ruin, employing terror and intimidation to undermine attempts at establishing a non-Communist central government in the area. With a new regime visibly supported by a majority of the populace and backed by sufficient force to extend its authority to wider areas of the country, the NLF will have to consider the attractions of political accommodation and the futility of prolonged violence. The present government in Saigon, as well as its successor, should do everything in its power to clear the path toward this objective. This objective can be served by increased emphasis on land reform, by drafting and enforcing eminently fair electoral laws, and by advancing the date of the presidential and legislative elections. I further believe that the present regime in Saigon should modify its extreme reluctance to discuss a political settlement with the National Liberation Front.

Political advancement in South Vietnam has been extraordinary. As I have indicated, I attended a session of the Constituent Assembly, and was present when South Vietnam's new constitution was finally adopted. I spoke with the President of the Assembly, Mr. Phan Khac Suu, who may well be a candidate for the presidency of all of South Vietnam, and with a number of Assembly members. I was impressed with their obvious sincerity, integrity, and skill. It is evident that, contrary to much American opinion, their delibera-

tions and decisions have been arrived at independently of political
pressures by the military junta which presently rules the country.
The so-called article 20, which authorized Prime Minister Ky and
the remainder of the directorate to amend the constitution prior to
its promulgation and which caused so much suspicion in this country, has not been used. Some suggestions made by the directorate
have been adopted by the Assembly; some, including ones on important issues, have been rejected. At no time has the Assembly
been overruled.

During the course of my conversations with Premier Ky, I tried
to impress upon him the necessity of permitting the Constituent Assembly to draft the electoral laws so that there would be more
broad public support for the elections. I am gratified to learn that
the directorate has agreed that the Constituent Assembly will enact
those laws. The entire process reflects an increasing political ma-
turity, and permits a good deal of optimism regarding an early
move away from military control and toward constitutional government.

The crucial question which is so deeply perplexing is what this
country must do to bring the conflict in Vietnam to a just conclusion. During the past twelve months, I have repeatedly argued that
the United States—which is so superior militarily and economically
to its opponent—ought to take the first step toward creating a better
climate for negotiations. I long debated whether to recommend
either a pause in the bombing of North Vietnam or some other
military de-escalation which might have persuaded Hanoi to enter
serious negotiations. With these thoughts in mind, I went to South
Vietnam to test their validity against the actual situation which I
would find there.

Everything I learned, not only in South Vietnam but also in
Japan, the Republic of China, the colony of Hong Kong, Cambodia and Thailand, has now convinced me that the enemy is not
disposed to participate in meaningful negotiations at this time. It
is the overwhelming consensus that the government of North Vietnam and the Vietcong leadership still doubt that the United States
will have the patience or fortitude to see this war to a successful

conclusion. No one with whom I conferred had at any time received any word or sign which might by the most generous interpretation be construed as an indication of Hanoi's willingness to negotiate. Those most familiar with the east Asian mentality in general, and the North Vietnamese mentality in particular, are convinced that the enemy still waits, still aspires to victory through collapse of the American will to persist.

How long this wait may be, how determined our effort must be before the enemy will be convinced of our steadfastness, is a matter of conjecture. It is possible that the North Vietnamese base their calculations on the expectation of a growing division in the American body politic on the question of our basic commitment in Vietnam. Oh, we may differ, Mr. President, on the conduct of the war. We may differ, and we do, on cessation or noncessation of bombing in the north. We may differ on whether to include the National Liberation Front in any possible negotiations. But, Mr. President, in the main the American people do not and have not differed on our basic commitment. And let there be no doubt in the mind of Ho Chi Minh or anyone else that the American people will persevere in their fundamental support of the South Vietnamese. That commitment is a willingness to discuss an equitable political settlement in Vietnam; and a readiness to continue our military and economic assistance to the South Vietnamese so long as is necessary.

The American people are beginning to accept, reluctantly but definitely, that this struggle could conceivably last another decade. On the other hand, there can be no doubt that the North has suffered severe losses during the past year and a half. The North Vietnamese-Vietcong casualty rate has continued to soar, and defections from their ranks have increased dramatically. Captured documents reveal that, by their own estimate, the Vietcong have lost control of a million people in recent months. It is possible that continued military pressure may end the war sooner than we dare to hope.

The reason for optimism is found in the high degree of dedication, morale, and combat efficiency which I observed among our fighting men. But I do not profess to attempt a prediction; and, indeed, I do not believe that others are in a position to do so.

Mr. President, I had hoped that a cessation of bombing in the north would bring about negotiations for peace, that if we did cease our bombing, Ho Chi Minh would come to the conference table and honest negotiations for peace could commence. I am discouraged by his recent statement affirming his original position that negotiations are impossible without cessation of bombing in the north coupled with a unilateral withdrawal of American and allied troops from South Vietnam. This reassertion of his original and fixed position shows no intention on the part of Ho Chi Minh to negotiate for peace at this time.

As a matter of fact, when I was in Cambodia I attempted through several intermediaries to talk with representatives of the Hanoi government. They were informed of my desire to talk and to understand the attitudes of the North Vietnamese government in regard to peace negotiations. The representative of the Hanoi government sent back a message that he believed that any discussions between us would serve no useful purpose at this time. After the Guam conference, Ho Chi Minh revealed a letter written by the President of the United States to him attempting to arrange a negotiated peace. Ho Chi Minh's answer was in substance the same as the answer that I received in Cambodia: that at this time Hanoi is not interested in negotiations or peace discussions. Ho Chi Minh continues to place unreasonable conditions on the negotiations for a peaceful settlement.

I believe the burden of responsibility has shifted from the United States, and shifted clearly to Hanoi. Thus, it does not appear that suspension of the bombing in the north would, by itself, produce fruitful negotiations. If, however, the time comes when the bombing seems to be a principal impediment to peace discussions, we should be prepared to cease bombing in the north.

Since I believe that North Vietnam is not prepared to negotiate in a meaningful way at this time, I must reluctantly conclude that the general direction of our present military efforts in Vietnam is necessary. This is far from an easy conclusion for me to reach. I know war. I am familiar with its consequences. I like to think of myself as a man who loves and desires peace for all men. But all too frequently what we desire and what reality thrusts upon us are very different.

I am convinced that human nature does not vary a great deal from continent to continent. I believe that Hanoi has its "hawks" and "doves" as does the United States. There must be factions in Hanoi who counsel restraint and an attempt at negotiation, as well as factions who advise continued attack in the hope of ultimate American withdrawal. I firmly believe that continuation of the war is based upon the influence of those in Hanoi who believe that the United States will falter in its basic commitment.

Mr. President, I do not intend my conclusions to suggest that I favor escalation of our military commitment in Vietnam. I do not advise military action which may arouse Communist China's fears that her borders are threatened and that her intervention is imperative. I do favor containment of the war within its present limited framework, and I advise patience until the enemy has finally concluded that a negotiated peace is the best and only solution.

The problems faced by the United States with respect to the country of Cambodia have been only slightly less complex than the problems posed in Vietnam. I believe that there is a general misconception on the part of the United States with respect to the position and objectives of the Cambodian people, and of their chief of state, Prince Norodom Sihanouk. I am most grateful to the distinguished majority leader, Senator Mike Mansfield, who is a close friend of Prince Sihanouk and who contacted the Prince through Cambodia's permanent representative to the United Nations in order to assist in arranging my visit.

The morning after my arrival in Phnom Penh, the capital of Cambodia, I was invited by Prince Sihanouk to attend a ceremony to inaugurate the opening of the bridge at Sangkum. Since the Prince had been in France from the beginning of January until early in March, this was his first opportunity to make a public statement with respect to the affairs of Cambodia and its international relations.

I was politely accorded a place of honor on the platform directly behind the Prince as he addressed a crowd of several thousand.

During his remarks, which were delivered in Cambodian, French, and partially in English, the Prince stated his esteem and good feeling for the American people, and expressed the belief that Ho Chi Minh undoubtedly felt the same way. He took pains to express his fondness and admiration for Senator Mansfield, for whom an avenue had been named in Cambodia. The Prince reiterated his familiar position that Cambodia did not wish to be a party to the ideological struggle between the East and West, but wanted simply to be left in peace to develop in its own way. He described his country's foreign policy as one of reciprocity—Cambodian attitudes toward other countries would depend primarily, even solely, upon the attitudes of such other countries toward Cambodian sovereignty and independence.

In the portion of the Prince's address which was delivered in English, he referred to the war in Vietnam as a civil conflict, which, in the beginning, could not have been considered a threat to world peace. Although he expressed his understanding why the United States might intervene in a controversy which really jeopardized the peace of the world, he insisted that United States intervention in the Vietnamese war had in fact created the very threat to world peace which the United States sought to avoid. He stated that American intervention had transformed a primarily internal controversy into a struggle of worldwide concern. At the conclusion of his remarks, we crossed the new bridge together, but there was no opportunity for me to present my own belief that the real threat to world peace had been posed by North Vietnamese aggression.

That evening a dinner in the name of the chief of state was given in my honor by the distinguished Mr. Son Sann, private counselor of the Prince. A number of prominent Cambodian officials were in attendance, including, besides Mr. Son Sann, the Secretary of State for Commerce, Mr. Seng Bun Korn; the Secretary-General of the Council of the Kingdom, Mr. Khieu Vann; the President of the Foreign Affairs Commission of the National Assembly, Mr. Keuky Lim; and members of the Foreign Affairs Ministry and the Ministry of Information. Also in attendance was His Excellency Noel St. Clair Deschamps, the Australian Ambassador to Cambodia, who was highly knowledgeable and most cooperative. Since the break in diplomatic relations between the United States and Cambodia, Mr. Deschamps has performed effective consular-type services in Cambodia for the United States Government.

The dinner lasted several hours, during which we conversed upon a number of subjects, especially questions relating to the foreign policy of Cambodia and to the reasons for the Cambodian-American rupture. Toward the close of the evening, I asked why Cambodia still retained diplomatic relations with Australia, despite Australia's participation in the war in Vietnam. Mr. Son Sann responded that participation in the war was a private matter for the Governments of the United States and Australia, and not the concern of Cambodia. He pointed out that the difference in the Cambodian view of the two countries was based upon the fact that at all times during the war Australia had respected the sovereignty of Cambodia and the inviolability of her borders, whereas he charged that the United States had clearly violated Cambodia's borders.

At the end of the dinner, Mr. Son Sann, in a short improvised address in English, stated that he was happy to receive me in the name of the Prince. He stated that he was pleased that I appeared to understand the Cambodian policy of strict neutrality which the Prince had defined earlier that day.

We hope—

Said Mr. Son Sann:

that your mission will contribute to the development of mutual understanding.

He added that Cambodia wishes to be left in peace to live in its own way. Said Mr. Son Sann:

The country not only loves peace, but needs peace in order to develop.

He concluded:

In conformity with our policy of strict neutrality, I would like to be friends with any country which respects us and considers us friends. It is the principle of reciprocity which is the basis of our foreign policy.

I responded by expressing in turn my gratitude to the Cambodian Chief of State for having invited me to attend the inauguration of the bridge, and for having indicated his good will to the citizens of the United States. I recognized Cambodia's desire for neutrality and the firm intention of the Prince to safeguard that neutrality. I said that I was happy to have visited Cambodia, and expressed the hope that if there had been any violations against the sovereignty of Cambodia, these would not be repeated.

I am convinced that the Cambodian people do not wish to be a part of the East-West power struggle. They have an understandable and completely justified desire to be left to live in their own way. Their conditions for resumption of diplomatic relations with the United States appear to be simple and sound.

Basically, they seek a sincere commitment by the United States that the territorial integrity of the Cambodian nation will not be violated. Although I know that United States commanders whose units operate along the Cambodian frontier have for the most part respected Cambodian sovereignty, there have been a number of unfortunate incidents in which troops have crossed the border and planes have flown over Cambodian territory. Perhaps the most unfortunate incident occurred at Thlok Trach, when American bombs were dropped upon a town which, for as long as all observers can remember, had been governed by Cambodia, although French maps located the town in South Vietnam. Such incidents give Cambodia cause to doubt American respect for Cambodia's sovereignty. Crossings of the border must be avoided if there is to be a restoration of diplomatic relations between the two countries.

It is most unfortunate that United States-Cambodian relations have reached the point where there is little or no communication. Mr. President, a truly neutral Cambodia is of great importance to the United States and to the peace of Southeast Asia. I would hope that the United States would seek practical ways to demonstrate to Cambodia its concern with its neutrality and its welfare.

The Mekong Committee has designated 1966 as Cambodia year, emphasizing assistance to that country. However, nothing has been accomplished, and this has proved to be a cause of great discouragement to Cambodians. Consideration should be given to providing a portion of the financing for the Prek Thnot Dam scheduled to be constructed by the international Mekong Committee with Cambodia. Cambodia was prepared at one time to accept American aid in connection with this project, but such aid was not provided. I believe that our position on this matter should be reconsidered, and that we should take advantage of an opportunity to show our friendship to the Cambodian people.

I would further hope that Prime Minister Ky's remarks on Guam on Tuesday of this week relating to Vietcong sanctuaries in Cambodia and supply trails in Laos would not be interpreted by these two countries as indicating that the United States or its allies has any intention whatsoever of violating their sovereignty. We should take strong steps to disassociate ourselves from such an implication. I believe that there should be a formal declaration by the Congress of the United States to the peoples of Cambodia and Laos assuring them that the United States entertains no intentions of involving either of them in the present conflict. We in this country must demonstrate that we are willing to do everything we can, and hope that the people of Cambodia will do everything they can, to reopen the channels of communication and of mutual understanding, leading to a resumption of diplomatic relations between Cambodia and the United States.

My trip ended in the country of Thailand, one of the strongest American allies in the region. The Thais are highly in favor of American participation in the war in Vietnam, feeling as they do that the entire region could conceivably be threatened by a Communist victory in that country. A number of persons with whom I conferred commented that every American indication of a possible cutback in the war effort is greeted by great anxiety in Thailand.

I believe that American economic aid to Thailand has been soundly conceived and effectively administered. We have worked in close cooperation with the Thai Government, and they are making full use of their own resources. Progress is steady, and the economy of the country is sufficiently sound that the Thais have been enabled to support more and more of their own economic development without external assistance.

As a result, a very large proportion—some 85 per cent—of American economic aid has been allocated to the area of counterinsurgency. The country is on the whole quite stable politically. But in recent years the northeast section has witnessed the rise of an insurgent group numbering about one thousand. The insurgents are, for the most part, Thais who are recruited by representatives of Peking or Hanoi to serve as a base for Communist development within Thailand. These people receive much of their political indoctrination from mainland China; but they are trained and equipped by Hanoi.

American response to the incipient insurgency in Thailand has, in my opinion, been well designed. We have not attempted to defeat the insurgency militarily. This is being handled by squads of elite Thai troops. We have provided through the AID program the economic assistance which is necessary to create a society in northeast Thailand in which insurgency cannot prosper.

We are helping the Thais create an atmosphere in which they can advance toward the goal of constitutional government. Although Thailand is presently ruled by a military government, personal freedom is enjoyed throughout the land. Without such personal freedom, the economic advancement of the past few years would have been impossible. A constitution is in the drafting stage and many observers feel that it may be promulgated before the end of the present calendar year. Thailand's measurable progress augurs well for the future.

The problems of the nations which I visited are so varied and complex that there is no single principle or set of principles which can be applied to all of them. It may well be that east Asia is not susceptible to any unified approach, but rather that different policies must be developed for each country. However, there are one or two factors which I believe are relevant to all of the nations of the regions, and I would like to conclude by referring to them.

Each area I visited, with the possible exception of Hong Kong—which is primarily a business community—has a strong sense of national identity. I believe this is true of all of the Asian nations. This is the indispensable fact for us to remember. Our policies must always take into consideration the fact that the countries of east Asia are concerned first and foremost—as well they should be—with their own destinies. Our task is to devise suitable arrangements for genuine and effective cooperation.

We must ever remain sensitive to the interests of the people who wish our assistance. We must make full use of those things which we do best. Our greatest strength is not force of arms. It is our political, economic, and technical capability. These assets can be far more effective in the long run than rifles and bombs. Totalitarian appeals thrive where people are without adequate food, clothing, housing, and education. It is obviously far better for the United States to assist in creating institutions and conditions which meet the needs of the people than it is to take arms to suppress unrest once it has occurred.

Finally, I believe that we must understand the limitations of the United States role in Asia. We have continuing responsibilities on that continent. But they are the responsibilities that any civilized nation has to assist countries which are less advanced and materially less fortunate. We do not have a responsibility to control the continent, nor to determine the ultimate destinies of all its inhabitants. We must seek less grandiose objectives, be they the economic development of countries like Thailand or Taiwan, or the gaining of an honorable peace in South Vietnam.

East Asia is a region of the world about which we know far too little. We are separated by great distances, as well as by differences in history, language, religion and, in many cases, an entire approach to life. But, whatever the differences, and whatever our policies are to be, I hope and pray that we never lose sight of the fact that we are dealing with millions of human beings preoccupied with the daily joys and burdens of their own lives, and anxious to determine their own destinies. I believe that ideas based upon a respect for these principles contain at least the germ of a sound policy—a human policy to govern our relations with this crucial part of the world.

THE CHANGING MONOLITH

THE IGNORANCE CURTAIN VS. THE OPEN DOOR [1]

George McGovern [2]

In a recent article in the *New Republic* entitled "Why Don't You Speak Out, Senator?" George McGovern, Democratic senator from South Dakota, expressed regret and a sense of frustration over the apparent failure of his and some of his colleagues' dissent in the Senate to influence our action in Vietnam. After referring to the efforts of Wayne Morse, Mike Mansfield, J. W. Fulbright, Robert F. Kennedy, and Ernest Gruening to change the Administration policy, Mr. McGovern ventured the opinion that the war might now be even larger, were it not for the persistent opposition of the critics. So he answered the question put in the title of the article by saying: "We have, and we can only pray that it has served some useful purpose."

Former director of the Food for Peace Program and former professor of history and political science at Dakota Wesleyan University, Mr. McGovern has been an articulate and outspoken critic of our actions in Southeast Asia. And he has voiced displeasure over the "meagerness of genuine discussion about fundamental issues" in public life. In his article "Foreign Policy and the Crisis Mentality" in the January 1967 *Atlantic*, he declared that "we are in danger of seeing the isolationists of the 1920's and 1930's replaced by the neo-imperialists who somehow imagine that the United States has a mandate to impose an American solution the world around."

In his address "The Ignorance Curtain vs. the Open Door," delivered before the United States Senate on May 3, 1966, Senator McGovern presented a historical-critical survey of our relations with China, and pleaded eloquently for a change of view—a new vision that would enable us to adapt our policy to the cataclysmic changes on the Asian continent:

> The obsession with communism that pulled us into the Vietnamese struggle has even more clearly dictated our policy toward China for the past two decades. In spite of the enormous power of the United States and the relative weakness of China, anticommunism has been a blinding light that has led us to aggravate the very dangers we most ought to diminish—the increased belligerence of China—the disruption of normal communications—a growing military involvement on China's border that could ignite a third world war.

[1] United States Senate, May 3, 1966. Text furnished by Senator McGovern, with permission for this reprint.

[2] For biographical note, see Appendix.

These convictions enjoy reasonably wide support. They echo the Fulbright thesis expressed in the speech "Old Myths and New Realities," delivered in the Senate on March 25, 1964, and his speech "The Two Americas," given at Storrs, Connecticut, March 22, 1966. Strong endorsement of the claim that the United States needs to take a new and hard look at our policy toward China came also from testimony at the special hearings on Southeast Asia before the Senate Foreign Relations Committee in 1966 and again in 1967.

Expressing the hope that we might break free from the "tyranny of slogans," and assuring his audience that a new course of action toward China would not endanger our security, Senator McGovern concluded:

> We have neither the mission nor the capacity to play God in Asia by a unilateral United States police operation. Vietnam should have taught us the futility of this role. But an enlightened United States policy that recognized China's reasonable diplomatic, economic and cultural interests might not only lessen Chinese belligerence; it would also be more inclined to win the approval of Japan, India, Pakistan, the Soviet Union and our Western European allies whose support will be required for any effective determination of China's legitimate role in Asia.

First Democratic senator from his state in more than two decades, Mr. McGovern shows his considerable rhetorical skills in this address. A former college debater at Dakota Wesleyan University, Mitchell, South Dakota, he was the recipient of a Pi Kappa Delta Distinguished Alumni Award in 1963.

"We must change to master change."

This little-noted phrase from President Lyndon Johnson's State of the Union Message of January 12, 1966, deserves a place in American state papers comparable to Franklin Roosevelt's "We have nothing to fear . . . ," John Kennedy's "Ask not what your country can do for you . . . ," and Dwight Eisenhower's warning of the growing "military-industrial complex . . . ."

Significantly, President Johnson advanced this concept in relation to domestic concerns—his plea for a "Great Society." The President was not, of course, calling for change merely for the sake of change; rather, he was suggesting that new challenges require new responses. Experiences as a youth growing up under difficult circumstances and long years in public life have led our President to reject the easy slogans which too many of us have accepted until recently. Notions such as "the unemployed are too lazy to work"—

"the Negro should stay in his place"—"old people who have not saved up for a rainy day deserve the poorhouse"—and other once accepted platitudes no longer serve the needs of a growing America. Instead, President Johnson speaks of a "Great Society" and reminds us that "We must change to master change."

In the enigmatic field of foreign policy, however, we have been slow to break free from the tyranny of slogans. While a changing world cries out for recognition that "We must change to master change," we are still guided in some areas by notions that have little relevance to present realities. If we are to avoid unrealistic crusades abroad that dissipate our moral and material strength, if we are to realize our dreams of a "Great Society," we must begin to apply the imaginative, up-to-date approaches to foreign policy that our President has brought to domestic concerns.

Nowhere has our failure to adapt policy to change been more apparent than in Asia—especially in China and Vietnam. If our painful and frustrating involvement in the Vietnamese conflict has finally triggered an examination of American policy in Asia, this could represent the one positive result from an otherwise melancholy venture. As one who questions some of the assumptions which have sent so many American troops to war in Southeast Asia, I believe that a fundamental reappraisal of policy is vital to our security as well as to the peace of the world.

The two most powerful forces moving in Asia since 1945 have been nationalism and the "revolution of rising expectations." With the collapse of the old British, French, Dutch and Japanese imperial systems during and after World War II, Asia was convulsed by revolutionary forces aimed at throwing off outside control and securing a better life for the people.

Our own revolutionary, democratic tradition enabled some Americans to understand these fundamental forces. Believing that Western imperialism had run its course by the end of World War II, our Government encouraged the British to liquidate their Asiatic colonial system; we insisted that Japan surrender her imperial holdings; we brought considerable pressure on the Dutch to withdraw from the East Indies; and we granted full independence to the Philippines.

But in China and Vietnam, the revolutionary leaders were Communists, which automatically made them the enemy in American eyes. To our policymakers, especially after the bitter experience of the Korean War, Mao Tse-tung and Ho Chi Minh were part of a worldwide Communist monolith bent upon global conquest. We seemed ready to ostracize any Communist government no matter how strong its base of local support, and to embrace any ally no matter how odious and ineffective, provided he carried an anti-Communist banner. Having substituted communism for the devil, we felt sufficiently free from sin to rebuke those who failed to enlist on the side of right. Although we had followed a policy of avoiding involvement in European alliances of the nineteenth century, Secretary of State Dulles regarded neutralism as "immoral" when practiced by the newly emerging governments of the post-World War II period. Forgetting that what we are *for* has been the source of our strength more than what we are *against,* we made anticommunism the guiding principle of our policy in Asia.

Thus, although Ho Chi Minh had stood with us in the war against Japan and saved American pilots shot down over the jungle, we backed the French effort to crush the Vietnamese independence struggle led by Ho. This action ran counter to President Franklin Roosevelt's view that Indochina should be placed under a UN trusteeship and prepared for independence. "France has milked it for one hundred years," Roosevelt said. "The people of Indochina are entitled to something better than that." But with his death, that view faded and two billion dollars in American aid went to the French effort which ended in defeat at Dien Bien Phu in 1954.

Ho Chi Minh emerged as a victorious hero from the eight-year war against France—not because he was a Communist, but because he tapped powerful forces of nationalism and popular revolution as a counter to a crumbling colonialism and an inept puppet regime. The evidence is convincing that if we had accepted Ho and permitted the Vietnamese to work out their affairs free from United States involvement, North and South Vietnam would have united under Ho. Such a regime might have served as a more effective buffer to Chinese penetration of Southeast Asia than the divided and warring two Vietnams which we helped initiate that have been the occasion for so much grief over the past decade.

However lofty our motives, Americans in Vietnam and the various political chiefs we have embraced in Saigon since 1954 have suffered from many of the same handicaps that plagued the French. As John King Fairbank puts it: "We are sleeping in the same bed the French slept in, but we are dreaming different dreams." In spite of enormous outlays of United States financial and military aid, it has been seemingly impossible to establish a government in South Vietnam capable of enlisting a dependable popular counterforce to the followers of Ho. Perhaps no one of the dozen regimes that have come and gone in Saigon in recent years could have stood without powerful United States props. Yet, the public embrace of a white Western power has also raised serious problems for the fleeting governments in Saigon, as General Ky has discovered in the Buddhist demonstrations. Given the current nationalistic sentiment of Asia, an American military embrace of the local politicians may embarrass and weaken them, while undercutting our own position. In Indonesia, for example, it was only after the American presence was diminished that local anti-Communist groups, freed from the charge that they were American stooges, took over and administered a severe setback to the pro-Chinese Communist forces.

We have supposed that the number one enemy of Asia was communism and that any sacrifice to contain it would be popular. But few Asiatics share our obsession with communism. The bad memories that fester in Asian minds are associated not with communism, but with Western imperialism and corrupt local hierarchies. The exploitative capitalism Asiatics have experienced bears little resemblance to the enlightened economy and public policies that have served America so well. So, while anticommunism has been an effective rallying cry to secure ever larger congressional authorizations of American military and financial aid for compliant regimes in Saigon and elsewhere, it has not been in tune with the strongest aspirations of the people of Asia. Too often we have become identified with corrupt, stupid and ineffective dictators who made the Communist revolutionists look appealing by comparison.

The obsession with communism that pulled us into the Vietnamese struggle has even more clearly dictated our policy toward China for the past two decades. In spite of the enormous power of the United States and the relative weakness of China, anticommunism has been a blinding light that has led us to aggravate the very dangers we most ought to diminish—the increased belligerence of China—the disruption of normal communications—a growing military involvement on China's border that could ignite a third world war.

Considering our sacrifices in World War II to save China from the Japanese, we were disappointed and alarmed by the collapse of Chiang Kai-shek before the Communist forces of Mao Tse-tung. This was an especially painful experience for Americans because we had prided ourselves on the "open door policy," our use of the Boxer Rebellion indemnities to finance Chinese students studying in the United States, our Christian missionary activity, and the Pacific war of the 1940's.

Americans blamed each other for "losing China"—forgetting that China was not ours to lose. Many Americans saw Chiang Kai-shek as a Christian statesman allied through his charming wife with the wealthy Soong family, devoted to justice and freedom. Actually, Chiang and the Soongs presided over a corrupt regime with little concern for the ordinary citizen. They mulcted both the United States aid program and their own people, while ruthlessly suppressing their critics. It was such a regime that paved the way for a Communist triumph.

The galling presence of a Communist government over the most populous nation on earth—especially a nation toward which we felt a peculiar paternalism—helps to explain why we almost literally closed our eyes on Chinese realities after 1949.

Instead of quickly recognizing the fact of Mao's government in Peking, we assisted the flight of Chiang to the island of Formosa and set him up as the recognized government of the nation that had just expelled him. There was some discussion in United States circles about recognizing the government in Peking, but such talk ended with the eruption of "McCarthyism" and the strident anti-communism of the early 1950's. A well financed "China lobby" skillfully cultivated American political, religious and military circles to secure maximum aid for Chiang and implacable opposition to the new government on the mainland.

Thus was forged United States policy toward mainland China —a policy based on the political, economic, diplomatic and psychological isolation of China combined with a bristling military containment. We have stoutly refused to recognize Peking and have blocked her entrance to the United Nations while insisting that Chiang's forces on the island of Formosa constitute the real Chinese government. No American trade has been permitted with mainland China, and we have tried strenuously to discourage other nations from trading with her. Travel by United States citizens, first-hand observation, study and reporting by our scholars and journalists, the exchange of scientific, cultural and entertainment personalities and works—all of these have been obviated by our non-recognition policy as well as by the bitter anti-Americanism of Peking.

If an "iron curtain" describes the barriers which separated the Soviet Union from the West in the postwar years, an "ignorance curtain" has descended between the United States and China since 1949. American ignorance of conditions in China is paralleled by even greater ignorance in China of the American people—of our concerns, our aspirations, our motives—although their leaders make certain that our faults are well-advertised. The lack of information and understanding based on normal exchanges is one of the most serious byproducts of the United States-China estrangement. Says China expert Doak Barnett: "There is less responsible public discussion in the United States of China policy than of any other foreign policy question of comparable importance." The meagerness of responsible public discussion is accented by the scarcity of competent China experts and researchers. Within the State Department, the McCarthy witchhunts of the 1950's took a heavy toll of competent, forthright specialists. Since then, State Department authorities have been largely muzzled by their fears of Congress while Congress has been muzzled by fears of the American public. The result is a paralysis of policy and a continuing ignorance that denies policymakers, the Congress, and our citizenry the opportunity to consider realistic alternatives.

The progression of the recent Senate Foreign Relations Committee hearings from the Vietnam issue to China policy has at long last focused public attention on the challenge of China. This may prove to be the most valuable service of Senator Fulbright and his committee.

In a complex policy area isolated for so many years from searching investigation and discussion, it will be difficult to devise acceptable new alternatives. No one of us has the competence to move with certainty in this long shrouded field. But our national interest as well as the peace of mankind demand that we open the curtain of ignorance with searching questions even if the answers are not immediately clear.

We need to ask whether it serves American security or world peace for us to ignore a nation that embraces a quarter of the world's people. Even if one assumes that the Chinese are trying to stab us in the back, the most dangerous stance would be to turn our back.

It may be contended, as has Secretary of State Rusk, that the Chinese have done much to isolate themselves. But does it really serve our interests to encourage Chinese isolationism through official American policy? Would it not make more sense from our point of view to revive the "open door"? Do Communist states evolve in a more moderate direction when they are deprived of diplomatic, cultural and economic relationships with the community of nations?

One wonders if nations, like individuals, do not become more hostile when they are ostracized by the community. History and elementary psychology would seem to point us toward policies designed to bring China into the family of man rather than to exclude her.

For sixteen years prior to 1933 we refused to recognize the Soviet Union. Since 1933 our relations with the Soviets have not been easy, but neither have they been entirely bad. We fought a great war as allies with the Russians from 1941 to 1945—a war that might have resulted in the triumph of Hitler over Western civilization had it not been for the enormous sacrifices of the Russian people. We have had many irritations and frustrations in our relations with the Soviets, but is there any responsible person who believes that Russia would have behaved more reasonably if she had been excluded from the United Nations, denied diplomatic recognition by the United States, and isolated economically and culturally from the West? The evidence is convincing that Russia's relationships with us and other nations have encouraged her more responsible position in world affairs. Soviet vetoes and speeches have often irritated us, but who would deny the beneficial impact of bringing Moscow under the subtle discipline of the United Nations family. Furthermore, as they have strengthened their own economy and society, the Russians have become less belligerent and ideological—more moderate and pragmatic.

This seems to be the historical pattern of revolutionary societies and may very well be true of the Chinese revolution. It is never easy to forecast the course of history, but of one fact we can be certain— men and nations change with the years. Today's enemies become tomorrow's allies. As Justice Holmes observed, "Time has upset many fighting faiths. . . ." History provides grounds for hope that the militant passions which now divide China and the United States may come into more balanced proportion with the passing of time. The Holy Crusades of the Middle Ages once enlisted the deepest emotions of Christians against the Moslems. But a modern authority, Sir Steven Runciman, looking back on this period, writes:

The triumphs of the Crusades were the triumphs of faith. But faith without wisdom is a dangerous thing. . . . There was so much courage and so little honor, so much devotion and so little understanding. High ideals were besmirched by cruelty and greed, enterprise and endurance by a blind and narrow self-righteousness; and the Holy War itself was nothing more than a long act of intolerance in the name of God, which is the chief sin against the Holy Ghost.

The lesson of the Crusades would seem to counsel, not another Holy War, but patience and restraint on our part while time works its way in the relations between China and the United States.

It may be argued that China is too aggressive to warrant membership in the international community. The growing bitterness between Russia and China might even lead the Russians to this view. There have been many belligerent, fanatical pronouncements from Peking and no one can fully comprehend Chinese behavior. Both Moscow and Washington are vilified daily—the United States being denounced alternately as a "paper tiger" and as an aggressor bent upon destroying China with the connivance of Moscow. Sino-Soviet expert Professor Donald S. Zagoria has noted that the Chinese bitterness toward Russia whom they regard as a traitor is more intense than their feeling about the United States whom they view simply as an enemy.

In any event, the gap between Chinese rhetoric and actual aggression is sufficiently wide to indicate that their bellicose utterances may be born more of fear and damaged pride than of any serious intent or capacity to conquer the world. The recent highly publicized document by Marshal Lin Piao—far from being a Chinese *Mein Kampf*—actually seems to be a warning to China's friends in Vietnam and elsewhere that they must fight their wars of liberation with little or no help from China.

In fact, Peking has been restrained and cautious in committing its military power abroad. Even in the Korean War, the Chinese did not enter until they saw American troops approaching their frontier after warnings that they would not tolerate this development. While sending "volunteers" into Korea, the Chinese refrained from the use of airpower.

In the 1962 border conflict with India, the claims of Peking were fully supported by the Nationalist Chinese government on Formosa and by some informed people in neutral states. When the Chinese armies pushed easily beyond the disputed area, they were quickly withdrawn to the line claimed by Peking as the legitimate boundary.

It is, of course, true that Peking is giving limited aid to North Vietnam and the Vietcong in the current Vietnamese war. But so far no Chinese soldiers are fighting in South Vietnam nor has Chinese airpower appeared, in spite of heavy and persistent American attacks close to the Chinese border.

At home, China is beset with enormous problems of too little food, too many people, and incredible difficulties of organization and development. She lacks the economic base, the food supply, the navy and the airpower to protect herself, to say nothing of waging a major war abroad.

None of this excuses China's belligerence—for example, her brutality in Tibet. It does, however, suggest that there is a considerable gap between the fire-eating pronouncements of the Chinese and their inclination or capacity to engage in overt aggression. While remaining alert to genuine danger signals from China, we would do well to remember Emerson's admonition: "Let him not quit his belief that a popgun is a popgun, though the ancient and honorable of the earth affirm it to be the crack of doom."

It should not be difficult to imagine that China is genuinely fearful of her present posture. She sees her former ally, the Soviet Union, moving into a cooperative relationship with the West. She sees the mighty American Seventh Fleet maneuvering constantly off her shores and fast-flying American planes bombing daily close to her frontiers. She sees Chiang with his 600,000-man army and air force backed by the United States still insisting that he will return to the mainland. She sees herself ringed by American nuclear installations capable of pulverizing her cities.

Heavily loaded United States bombers are poised on bases in Formosa, Okinawa, Japan, the Philippines, Thailand, and South Vietnam. Remembering our frightened and angry reaction to the installation of Russian missiles in Cuba in 1962, it should not be difficult for us to understand China's reaction to the ring of United States nuclear power that confronts her. What would be our attitude if enormous Chinese air power were pointed at us from bases in Mexico City, Montreal, Staten Island, and Bermuda?

This kind of "containment" invokes painful Chinese memories of a century of humiliation and exploitation at the hands of the Western powers. Beginning with the Opium Wars of the 1840's the European states, including Czarist Russia, ruthlessly carved out areas of exploitation in China that were sealed with "the unequal treaties." This was an especially traumatic experience for the Chinese because of their deeply rooted sense of cultural superiority.

"This humiliation," writes China observer Charles Taylor, "still deeply felt, helps to explain the curious mixture of concern and defiance with which China regards the military power now ranged around its borders."

The triumph of the Communists in 1949 ended Western exploitation, but Chinese leaders bear the scars not only of a century of shame; they especially recall America's effort in the recent past to crush them in their struggle with Chiang Kai-shek. Now they see their country surrounded by massive American power while their former ally, the Soviet Union, has apparently deserted them.

Chinese foreign policy is aimed at the diminution of United States military power in Asia, the annexation of China's former territories—especially Formosa, and the acceptance of China as a great power. In effect, China would like to establish a Monroe Doctrine that would give her the kind of role in Asia which we proclaimed for ourselves in the Western Hemisphere. The Chinese mistakenly expected the Russians to back up their objectives much as the British fleet supported the Monroe Doctrine for us during the nineteenth century.

Peking's current goals would doubtless be pursued by any strong Chinese government—Communist or non-Communist. The evidence is compelling, however, that China will not recklessly commit her military power.

But even if one accepts Chinese belligerence at face value—even if China has done much to isolate herself, and even if she repeatedly spurns United States initiatives toward improved relations, I believe that American policy should now be pointed toward achieving a reconciliation with the people and the government of this vast country. The United States is great enough and powerful enough and wise enough to take the lead during the next decade or two in modifying the bitterness and fear that have developed between China and ourselves.

A first step in that direction should be a careful examination accompanied by public discussion of all aspects of our China policy.

There is no more urgent responsibility confronting American scholars, journalists, members of Congress and government officials than a reexamination and restructuring of Sino-American relations. A problem so important to ourselves, our children, and all mankind should be analyzed and discussed with candor and with courage. Senator Fulbright has helped to set us on that course by the stimulating investigation recently conducted by his committee.

The discussions launched by the Senate Foreign Relations Committee should be broadened and pursued in depth. To strengthen that effort, I would suggest that the President name a blue-ribbon China commission of highly qualified Americans headed perhaps by former President Eisenhower or Generals Ridgway or Gavin. Such a commission could look carefully at the various aspects of United States-China relations and recommend needed policy changes or initiatives.

A distinguished commission of this kind would have the authority and prestige to marshal the finest talent in the nation and make their views known to the American people. Qualified men specializing on China are sadly lacking in the State Department although there are a handful of highly able experts there as well as in some of our great universities. But such brilliant men as George Kennan, Charles Bohlen and Llewellyn Thompson—experts on Soviet affairs—are not easily found in the China section of the State Department. We need to be about the business of developing such men and harnessing their talent as quickly as possible.

Second, China should be invited to participate in the disarmament and nuclear proliferation talks at Geneva. This suggestion, advocated by Senator Robert Kennedy and others, is clearly in our national interest. If we believe that China is a potentially dangerous nuclear power, it makes little sense to exclude her from conferences designed to bring some degree of control over nuclear weapons. It is not clear that Peking would accept an invitation to participate in such discussions, but after the explosion of her first nuclear device she suggested a global conference on nuclear control and disarmament which we promptly rejected. It might be worth while for some of the neutral nations to initiate a dialogue aimed at reviving this proposal and drawing the Chinese into a significant role.

Third, we should drop our opposition to the admission of China to the United Nations. We need not become an advocate of Peking's admission, but neither should we try any longer to pressure other nations into voting against admission. China may be voted a seat in the United Nations this fall no matter what we do. But this is a matter for the member nations of the United Nations to decide free from undue pressures from the United States or other great powers. Certainly, we should not use our foreign assistance program as an indirect device to buy votes in the General Assembly against the admission of mainland China. Foreign assistance is too costly and serious a business to waste on a lost cause. It is not clear that Peking would accept a seat in the United Nations, but this is not relevant to the basic question of whether or not she should be offered admission.

Fourth, while encouraging self-determination for the people of Formosa, we should indicate our willingness to abide by the judgment of the United Nations as to a possible solution for the Formosan problem. This is the issue that bars serious discussion of China's relationship to both the United Nations and the United States. Both Communist China and Chiang's Nationalist regime insist that there is only one China of which Formosa is a part. The Nationalists now hold Formosa as well as the Chinese seat in the United Nations and insist that Peking must not be recognized or admitted to the United Nations. Peking, on the other hand, insists that Chiang has no legitimate claim to either Formosa or mainland China and must be expelled from the United Nations before Peking will enter.

The immediate origin of the Formosa problem was the Cairo Conference of 1943 at which President Roosevelt and Winston Churchill promised Chiang Kai-shek that Formosa would be given to China after the defeat of Japan. The island had been ceded to Japan "in perpetuity" by the Chinese at the end of the Sino-Japanese war in 1895. During the next half century of energetic Japanese rule, Formosa became a developed society with a sense of identity apart from the Chinese mainland. The Formosans eagerly anticipated the end of Japanese rule in the expectation that they would have a more effective political voice in their own affairs as a part of postwar China.

Instead, Chiang's government immediately suppressed all overtures from the Formosans toward representation in the government that emerged after 1945. Formosan political leaders were imprisoned or executed and the island was invaded by hordes of opportunists from the Chinese mainland who appropriated all the property that could be carted off or exploited for private gain. Formosan residents, as distinct from those who came from China after World War II, were excluded from all important political, commercial and educational positions.

When Chiang was defeated by the Communists in 1949, he and two million supporters fled to Formosa and made the island their fiefdom—ignoring the wishes of the ten million residents. Heavily supported by United States military and economic aid, Formosa has prospered economically, although to this day it knows little democracy. Many of its people, including some who came from China after 1949, now feel the same kind of separate identity from the Chinese mainland that developed during the half century of Japanese rule. There is considerable evidence that Chiang's professed determination to return to the mainland is not shared by many of his subjects. Meanwhile, it seems ironical that the peace of the world is jeopardized by the uncertain status of this little island.

Our only honorable way out of the Formosa dilemma is to foster a situation of self-determination there combined with a more active United Nations role aimed at an acceptable solution. We cannot lightly turn Formosa over to Peking since that would be a betrayal of both the Chinese who fled there after 1949 and of the Formosans' hope for a hand in their own governance. Neither can we hope to maintain permanent credibility for the fiction that

Chiang will recover control of mainland China from his island base.

Peking can be expected to oppose any arrangement that does not simply turn the island over to her. Chiang will object to any proposed election supervised by outsiders on the grounds that it would represent meddling in the internal affairs of Formosa. The Nationalist regime has never had a popular mandate, although it has developed an election process in local administration under the Formosa Provincial Government. We should applaud this development and put our influence behind any and all procedures that permit the people of Formosa to determine their own government and in time establish their independence by democratic means.

Should not the Formosa Provincial Government begin to play a greater role in administration of the island's economic affairs? Should we not expect the Nationalist government and the Provincial government eventually to merge in the interests of greater efficiency and responsiveness to popular interests? Aging President Chiang, through his controlled Nationalist legislature, has just appropriated increased power, assumed another six-year term, and designated his successors. These are decisions that should ideally be made by the people of Formosa in genuine elections.

If our moral support of the election process is accompanied by a clear reaffirmation of our commitment to defend the island, it could not be charged that we were abandoning our allies and the containment of mainland China. We should make clear that we will not tolerate Chinese aggression, nor would we ever permit Chiang and his Nationalist followers to be handed over to Peking. Nationalist mainlanders and Formosans alike should equally enjoy the rights of citizenship in an independent, democratic Formosan state. In such a situation, the world could see that self-determination was a fact because all the people on Formosa could participate in full political life.

Since our policy toward Formosa has been widely questioned in the international community, it would be wise for us to place the entire issue before the United Nations. We could indicate our willingness to abide by the decisions of the Assembly with the understanding that the wishes of the Formosans would be considered and that adequate security arrangements would be worked out. This would place on the members of the United Nations the responsibility for finding an acceptable answer to the Formosan dilemma rather than creating the impression that America is blocking a solution. We should make clear that we are willing to live not only with a "One China" or "Two Chinas" policy, but that we would be happy to see a "One China-One Formosa" solution with maximum self-determination for the people of Formosa.

Aside from such diplomatic questions as the recognition of China, her entrance to the United Nations, and the status of Formosa, there are a number of other areas in which United States initiatives might encourage a better relationship between ourselves and the Chinese.

In April 1965 the United States Chamber of Commerce unanimously called upon our Government "to more effectively open channels of communication with the people" of mainland China. United States Chamber President Robert Gerholz, who favors trade, discussion and cultural exchange with the Chinese, said at that time: "It makes no sense for the United States not to be in touch with a country of 700 million people." He added: "Any time you can get people around a conference table . . . I prefer it to bombing and going to war."

In that spirit, we could encourage an exchange with China of scholars, journalists, businessmen, artists, educators, farmers, scientists, and tourists. Both China and the United States could profit from an exchange of scientific and technical information in such fields as weather modification, population control, agricultural development, and medical research. Such a policy would avoid the kind of foolish decision that recently prevented us from accepting a rare Chinese panda bear that a friendly Australian wished to donate to an American zoo. One wonders if Chinese pandas would really infect us with a dangerous Communist virus!

President Johnson acted wisely in his recent decision to permit American scholars to study in China and to grant visas to Chinese scholars applying for study in the United States. Whether or not

Peking will admit our scholars or grant passports to her scholars in the immediate future is questionable, but at least we have taken a first step toward opening the ignorance curtain.

Specifically, I would suggest that two or more of our great universities, perhaps Harvard and the University of California, and two or more institutions of higher learning in neutral countries assemble a task force of medical or other specialists and offer through the neutralist universities to send them to China on an exchange basis.

The Pugwash group of scholars that have had such striking success in establishing private technical communication with their Soviet counterparts, even during the roughest cold war period, might be asked to apply themselves to reaching Chinese scholars on terms not offensive to Peking.

Institutions such as South Dakota State University or Iowa State University might be asked to host a conference on agricultural problems and techniques to which Chinese experts could be invited along with other participants. These universities are so located that visits to nearby farms would give the Chinese observers an opportunity to communicate directly with our farmers and view the operation of typical American farms.

We could emphasize our willingness to increase communications with the Chinese by eliminating the requirement of special passports to China and other nations. Any adult citizen should be allowed to travel at his own discretion whenever he can secure a visa. The right to travel should be a basic right of American citizens.

For a time prior to 1960, Peking seemed to be interested in negotiating an exchange of newsmen with the United States. Since then, the Chinese have said that progress on this and other issues must await settlement of the Formosan problem. Some fifty United States journalists have validated passports for China, but only Edgar Snow and a farm expert who was inadvertently issued a visa in Helsinki have been admitted. For the United States to drop the travel ban on all citizens would make our own principles clearer and more confident while placing the responsibility on Peking for roadblocks to communications and travel.

We should open the door for trade in nonstrategic materials and cease our pressures to discourage other nations from trading with the Chinese. Sixty-eight per cent of China's trade is now with our "free world" allies. Japan has replaced Russia as China's major trading partner—an arrangement that benefits both Japan and China and makes China less dependent on the Communist world.

Since no responsible Chinese official has proposed increased trade with the United States, there is no immediate likelihood of a flourishing trade with us. But the removal of present blanket prohibitions would enable individual U.S. traders to deal with China much as they have with Russia and Eastern Europe. Today, the only goods that cross borders are publications and printed material between libraries and various institutes, but this trickle might flow faster if present United States regulations were relaxed so that we might trade with the Chinese on the same basis as we do the Russians.

This would not weaken American security but it could introduce China's agricultural and industrial managers to American goods and methods. It could stimulate demands among their engineers and technicians for greater access to U.S. technical data. It could open the door for sales of wheat and other surplus crops to a nation which undoubtedly contains many hungry mouths.

In recent years China's fast-growing population, unfavorable weather, and the failure of the "great leap forward" have resulted in large grain shortages. As a consequence, Peking has purchased huge quantities of wheat and other cereals from Canada, Australia, and France. Indeed, Canadian farmers and exporters are experiencing an economic boom as a result of sizable sales to China and the Soviet Union. The Canadian, Australian and French governments have relaxed acreage controls, utilized surpluses, and stimulated their agricultural and related industries. The Chinese grain purchases have been a new-found gold mine to our wheat exporting allies.

The United States, in contrast, is struggling to control the output of farmers by acreage controls, land retirement schemes, and other expensive devices. We have sought to isolate our accumulated surpluses in government-financed storage programs. While putting up with tight acreage restrictions and price depressing surpluses, farmers have been blamed for the high public cost of the control program. Meanwhile, the entire economy has suffered from a restricted and depressed agriculture.

Given these factors, would it not be in the nation's interest to lift some of the restrictions that have foreclosed U.S. grain sales in China and other parts of the Communist world? Is there really any reason to believe that a well-fed Communist is more dangerous than a hungry one?

Such trade would obviously be of economic benefit to us in increased income and a sharply improved balance of payments. If the political blocks to trade could be removed, American farmers could expect to sell a quarter of a billion dollars of grain to the Chinese each year. This would not only enrich our farmers, it would mean new economic stimulus and greater sales of farm machinery, farm supplies, shipping and materials of all kinds. Idle acres and abandoned farms would once again begin to produce and rural communities would feel strengthened purchasing power. The potential impact of a flourishing trade with a nation approaching a billion people is difficult to comprehend. Such trade is also a sound political and moral position for the nation in demonstrating the efficiency of our agriculture and industry and our recognition that even political rivals should not be denied food and other nonstrategic materials which we have in abundance that they might be willing to purchase.

The foregoing are a few of the steps which the United States could take with no serious risk that might strengthen our security by encouraging more amicable relations with the people of China. They would not lessen the effective military containment of China, but might in fact make it more practical. We have neither the mission nor the capacity to play God in Asia by a unilateral United States police operation. Vietnam should have taught us the futility of this role. But an enlightened United States policy that recognized China's reasonable diplomatic, economic and cultural interests might not only lessen Chinese belligerence; it would also be more inclined to win the approval of Japan, India, Pakistan, the Soviet Union and our Western European allies whose support will be required for any effective determination of China's legitimate role in Asia.

The suggested steps should make clear that while we would resist any military aggression by the Chinese, we want to see them prosper in a climate of peace. While we do not approve of their system of government for ourselves, we could wish them continued progress in their efforts to organize and develop their vast country and conquer its staggering problems. The Chinese have accomplished much of value in a few short years—improving the status of women, lifting the educational level of the people and eliminating most of the crime, prostitution, and corruption of their great cities. In spite of droughts, floods, heavy population pressures, and organizational mistakes, they have vastly improved their food distribution so that large-scale starvation has been prevented. Scientific, technical and economic advancements have been remarkable. All of these worth-while accomplishments, achieved without substantial aid from other countries, are worthy of our respect. It is true that they have been accompanied by a high degree of regimentation, but as Professor Lucian W. Pye has observed: "The mere assignment of ruling what may become half the world's population with only a small fraction of the world's resources will compel Chinese leaders to keep their society on a tight leash."

It is not likely that China would respond favorably to United States initiatives in the immediate future. Her leaders are not presently in a happy mood. China's heavy-handed interference in Africa, Indonesia and Cuba has been rebuffed by the people of those states which she thought were logical allies. She has suffered a bitter estrangement from the Soviet Union. Aside from the deep scars of a century of Western humiliation, her leaders are haunted by the memories of the "Long March" and decades of civil strife and misrule. They bitterly resent the United States nuclear power that encircles them—to say nothing of the escalating war in Vietnam.

For these and other reasons, China may react in a hostile, if not hysterical manner to United States overtures. UN Secretary-General U Thant has said that the Chinese leadership is gripped by the anxieties of a nervous breakdown. If that analysis is correct, it is all the more urgent that we take reasonable steps to quiet their fears. Certainly, we will not make China less belligerent by answering hysteria with hysteria, or name calling by name calling. When the Chinese recite our faults and ignore our virtues, it does not make them more reasonable for us to display the same blind emotionalism. If they have a distorted image of us, that does not make it in our interest to live with a distorted vision of them.

We must be prepared for rebuffs, insults and misinterpretations of our motives. But with enough patience, an imaginative policy aimed at drawing China into the family of nations should bear more fruit than a policy designed to isolate, antagonize and hamper her development.

As the exponents of freedom, we would do well to remember the words of Judge Learned Hand: "The spirit of liberty is the spirit which is not too sure that it is right; the spirit of liberty is the spirit which seeks to understand the minds of other men and women; the spirit of liberty is the spirit which weighs their interests alongside its own bias. . . ."

Senator Fulbright has brilliantly highlighted the danger of following "old myths" rather than "new realities." If, however, one considers current tendencies to substitute military power and diplomatic rigidity for the eternal imperatives of brotherhood and reconciliation, it may be that our *dilemma* stems from substituting new myths for old realities.

But regardless of the angle of vision on our growing quandary in Asia, we need to develop that reasonableness of mind, that "spirit of liberty," which gives force to the words: "We must change to master change."

STATEMENT BEFORE THE
SENATE FOREIGN RELATIONS COMMITTEE [3]

EDWIN O. REISCHAUER [4]

Vietnam continues to be a prime enigma of our time. Despite numerous and occasionally hopeful reports of peace movements or at least peace talks, the conflict goes on, indeed becomes more ominous. And many responsible men and women disagree profoundly on the course the United States should follow. Perhaps the one point on which there is fullest agreement, as Edwin O. Reischauer recently remarked in a magazine article, is "that it is something we should have avoided." He went on to say, however, that the alternative actions are few and unsatisfactory, making the policy of limited warfare about the best available.

Understandably, many Americans are preoccupied with the immediate problem in Vietnam. But it is only a part of the capacious context of Southeast Asian relations and of our transactions with the Communist world. The principal Asian figure on this global set is of course China. During late January 1967, the Senate Foreign Relations Committee turned again to what *Newsweek* has called "Senator J. William Fulbright's seminar on American foreign policy," this time to assess our posture in Asia and to determine whether or not our dealings with the Communist nations and with the underdeveloped states are compatible with political realities. Testifying before the Committee were distinguished and knowledgeable men. There was historian Henry Steele Commager, who felt that America was obsessed with the messianic notion of spreading its ideological principles throughout the globe. Commented Professor Commager: "Justice Holmes used to say that the first lesson a judge had to learn was that he was not God. It is a lesson every man has to learn, and a lesson every nation has to learn. . . ." This view is not unlike the one held by Walter Lippmann, who, remarking on the Manila Conference in late November 1966, said the Administration's policy was based on a fallacy; it did not take into account "the cataclysmic consequences of the collapse of the empires and of the decolonialization of the enormous land masses of the Asian continent." Also appearing before the Senate Foreign Relations Committee was Harrison Salisbury, assistant managing editor of the New York *Times,* the first American newsman to report from North Vietnam since we became actively involved in the war. George Kennan, former

[3] Washington, D.C., January 31, 1967. Text furnished by Mr. Reischauer, with permission for this reprint.

[4] For biographical note, see Appendix.

ambassador to Russia, testified that the notion of the so-called Communist monolith is no longer realistic; Communist lands are shaping their destinies along distinctively nationalistic lines. They are no longer a "single disciplined force." "The unity of the Communist bloc is a matter of the past; and it will not be restored. This Humpty-Dumpty will not and cannot be reassembled."

Another witness before the Committee was Edwin O. Reischauer, Harvard professor and former ambassador to Japan, who voiced a similar view. We have, he asserted, "overreacted to images in our own minds and underreacted to the actual historical tides of Asia. Monolithic conspiracy has little future in the soil of Asia's diversity."

Mr. Reischauer's speech, delivered on January 31, 1967, and reprinted below, is an excellent model for critical study. Like Mr. Kennan's statement on Vietnam before the same committee in 1966 (reprinted in REPRESENTATIVE AMERICAN SPEECHES: 1965-1966, pages 56-65), Mr. Reischauer's address is a closely reasoned, severely organized set of ideas. A man of enormous experience and insight into Asian affairs, he gives to his words an indelible stamp of credibility and authority. Because of the nature of the audience—a select, prestigious committee and visitors who crowded the chamber—the speaker made little or no effort to adapt the message to the emotional climate of the time. Instead, he dealt largely in exposition and argument, and in the revelation of political concepts issuing from the interpretations. Students of public address will find here a suitable example of effectively interlaced logical and ethical persuasion.

It is a great privilege to appear before this distinguished committee and, at the same time, a heavy responsibility. The subject you have asked me to comment on—"Asia, the Pacific and the United States"—is so vast and complex that no one can claim more than a very limited view of the whole. I shall attempt, however, to be responsive to your request and to the specific questions raised in the preliminary memorandum which was sent to me. Since I must cover so large a subject in such brief compass, I will have to speak in broad generalities, without the benefit of careful qualifications and subtleties of distinction. I regard my role in this hearing as being to provoke discussion, rather than to provide definitive solutions.

Asia, as I see it, is likely to be the area of our most difficult foreign policy decisions, not only in the immediate future but for many decades to come. This is not surprising, because even that restricted part of Asia which stretches from Pakistan and India eastward to China and Japan contains over half the population of the world; most of the people in this area live in underdeveloped and therefore relatively unstable countries: and our knowledge of these lands, both within the Government and in the public at large, is probably less adequate than in the case of any other major part of the world.

Knowledge, of course, cannot be equated with wisdom, but knowledge certainly is a prerequisite to sensitive understanding, which in turn is necessary for wisdom in policy. I believe very strongly that we in this country must put greater emphasis on learning more about the countries and societies of Asia, both in terms of specialized knowledge and in terms of popular understanding. We also need to make a conscious effort to inject more expert knowledge of Asian affairs at the high, policy-making levels of the Government, in order to help balance the much greater degree of knowledge of the West that exists among our leaders. Until we have done both these things, we stand, I believe, on dangerously thin ice in our approach to the manifold, perplexing problems of our relationship with Asia.

The situation in Vietnam seems to me a case in point. I am myself a supporter of the Administration's objective in Vietnam, which, as I understand it, is to bring the war to as speedy an end as possible, without resorting to either of the dangerous alternatives of withdrawal or major escalation. I might add that, in my view, this objective can best be attained by prudent de-escalation of the conflict's purely military aspects—for instance, the bombing of the North. Regardless of how one views our present policy, however, I believe we would all agree that our position in Vietnam is something we should have avoided. If at several times in the past we had correctly judged the realities of the situation in Vietnam, the risks involved, and the limitations of our influence, we would have made different choices than we did. Decisions, which at the time may have seemed small and relatively unimportant, led us step by step to our present unhappy position. My personal feeling is that two of our major mistakes were made early—in the years after 1945 in backing the revival of French colonialism and in 1954 in stepping into the unsound situation the French left behind them. Be that as it may, the war in Vietnam shows that we need a clearer concept of our long-range relationship with Asia so that we will have sounder guide lines in the day-to-day decisions that cumulatively shape our policy.

We have in the past, I believe, frequently applied to Asia attitudes and policies developed in our relations with Europe, without taking into adequate consideration the vast differences between the two areas. We have tended to equate the threat that the Soviet Union posed to the independence of the countries of Europe with quite dissimilar threats to stability and independence that the Asian countries faced. We have sought to meet these threats in Asia with the same system of alignments and firm defense lines that proved successful in Europe, even though the vast areas and populations involved, the weakness of the local economies, the instability of political institutions, and the psychological and cultural barriers between us and Asians made such alignments and defense lines much less effective and much harder to maintain than in Europe.

I do not, however, subscribe to the thesis that there are some fundamental differences between our Atlantic and Pacific relationships based on geography or the different cultural backgrounds of the trans-Atlantic and trans-Pacific areas. Nor do I believe in a sharp distinction between our role as a Pacific power and as an Asian power. There are, of course, differences in the distances to Europe, to the western edge of the Pacific, and to the Indian subcontinent that are important even in this day of rapid global movement. Because of our preponderant naval power, islands remain more defensible than continental areas. And cultural differences are naturally very important in international relations. But in this rapidly shrinking world, our fundamental foreign policies, I believe, must be worldwide. Within the limits of our power and influence, we must seek to achieve peace, stability, prosperity and the right to national self-determination everywhere, or we may end up by achieving these goals nowhere.

There are, however, differences in how these goals are best pursued in different parts of the world. One distinction in our foreign policies that I believe must be recognized clearly is the difference between our relationship with the modernized, industrialized nations and with the so-called less-developed regions. This is more a temporal difference than a geographic or cultural one. It derives from the time lag in the acquisition of modern technology and institutions on the part of the less-developed nations. The industrialized countries enter significantly into the immediate balance of power in the world, both military and economic; the less-developed lands are economically deficit areas and have little but strictly localized military power. The former, for the most part, are divided between countries which share with us much the same liberal, democratic traditions and institutions and those that are organized along Communist lines; the less-developed lands are mostly countries in flux, seeking to establish a fixed pattern but far from having achieved one. The advanced nations are internally stable and need only fear external pressures; the less-developed countries are, for the most part, far more threatened by internal instability than by external aggression. In the former, defense lines, such as we can help erect, stand on a firm foundation of advanced economies and stable institutions, while our economic aid or cooperation can be immediately effective; in the latter our type of military power sinks all too easily into a quagmire of economic and political disruption, and economic progress is a slow, uncertain process. Judging from the case histories of India, Burma, Indonesia and Vietnam, the nationalistic ardor of the less-developed countries may give them greater security against foreign domination and internal subversion than do military alliances and foreign military aid. This, in particular, is a lesson we should keep in the forefront of our minds as we deal with Asia.

Obviously, the problems of the developed and less-developed nations are quite dissimilar. Most important, we must approach them with entirely different time scales in mind. The aggressive capacities or needs for defense of the industrialized nations are matters of immediate concern to the United States. These countries can be dangerous enemies or effective allies right now. The momentary situation or attitudes of the less-developed countries are of less vital concern to us. As allies, they may detract more from our over-all strength than they add to it. As enemies, they threaten few if any of our vital interests. What really counts is how they develop over the next several decades, as they modernize their technology and institutions and develop power. Will they become healthy, stable members of a peaceful world order; or, will they, through their own instability or aggressiveness, militate against it?

There is another important distinction between our relationship with the industrialized nations and the less-developed ones. The latter for the most part have emerged only recently from colonialism or semicolonial conditions. This makes them far more sensitive and apprehensive in their relations with us than are the industrialized nations. Even with the latter, our great size and power cause problems. At least I found this to be the case in our contacts with Japan during my years there as ambassador. With the less-developed countries, the situation is far more difficult. They see us, not just as a superpower, but as the greatest of the Western nations that until recently held colonial sway over much of the world. We are heirs—however innocently or unwittingly—to a bitter history of humiliation and exploitation by the Western powers. Not unnaturally they fear our domination, resent our great influence, and often bridle at our leadership. However good our intentions, our exercise of power and influence in these countries is all too likely to clash with their strong sense of nationalism. This is all the more true in areas like Asia, where basic differences in race and cultural background underscore the contrast in technological advancement and power between us and them. There is a distinctiveness to the civilizations of Asia that makes our every move in Asia more intrusive than in areas culturally or technologically more akin to us. For these reasons we must bring to our Asian relationships a special degree of caution, restraint, and modesty in the exercise of our power.

Another major consideration in trying to come to grips with the problems we face in Asia is our estimate of what in general lies in store for that part of the world. Are the countries of Asia growing in viability or are they becoming less stable? Are they becoming

more susceptible to internal subversion and aggression from abroad
or less so? Are international communism and Chinese neo-imperial-
ism growing or fading menaces? We must face questions such as
these and answer them as best we can, before we can make any clear
judgments about alternative United States policies.

My own personal reading in all these matters is on the optimistic
side. However slow the progress in most of Asia, the general movement, I feel, is upward economically and toward more viable political and social systems. The threat of unitary world communism
sweeping Asia has largely faded, and the menace of Chinese domination—if ever it was a real menace in the military sense—is growing weaker. Almost all of the countries of Asia are gaining in
national cohesiveness and in confidence. In some areas there has
been encouraging progress toward the development of a healthy
sense of regional cooperation. Some of these things may be happening because of our Vietnam stance, but fundamentally they are happening for other more basic reasons and in some cases despite our
stand in Vietnam. If the present Vietnam crisis can be solved without either great escalation or a headlong retreat by the United States,
I believe that we can count on the situation in Asia continuing
slowly to improve, rather than deteriorating.

Another problem in attempting to define what our Asian policies
should be is the size and the diversity of the area concerned. Asian
nations neither are alike nor act alike. Each is very distinctive. I
therefore doubt that blanket policies should or could be applied to
all of the countries of Asia. Some, because of strategic location or an
important product, are of more immediate concern to us than
others. As examples, I might cite the vital sea routes through the
Straits of Malacca and the oil of west Asia. As I have said, we can
offer effective defense more easily to island countries than to continental ones. Some countries more eagerly seek relations with us
than others, and with some we have developed special bonds. The
Philippines, South Korea and Taiwan are cases in point. Most
important, some countries are far closer to being stable, modernized
nations than are others.

In this regard, Japan is, of course, a special case. Not so much because it is an island nation or a Pacific, as opposed to an Asian, land, but because it is a thoroughly modernized country. Japan, I believe, is as much a natural partner and ally of the United States as any country in Europe. The Japanese have a stable society, not susceptible to subversion or vulnerable to guerilla warfare. They are capable of great economic influence in the rest of the world, particularly in Asia, and, if they so chose, they could be a significant part of the world balance of military power. They share with us much the same sort of life and have the same general international interests and aspirations. I find our present mutual security relationship with Japan and all our other forms of close cooperation entirely sound. I would expect these ties to grow stronger rather than weaker in the future. As other Asian nations achieve a comparable degree of modernization, I would also expect some of them to develop comparable forms of partnership with us. For the time being, however, Japan remains a case by itself, to be considered as an exception to almost all the generalizations about Asia and our policy toward Asia.

Returning to the other Asian lands, I should like to put forward, on the basis of the broad concepts discussed above, a few general propositions, as indicative of the fundamental directions in which we should be trying to move over the years ahead. I cannot in the format of this brief presentation explore these propositions fully, but I believe they are concepts which should be studied carefully. Stated bluntly and with a minimum of justification or explanation, these propositions are:

1. We should seek to minimize our military involvement and military commitments in Asia, because our vital interests are not likely to be threatened in most of Asia, because our type of military strength is not very effective in meeting subversion and guerrilla warfare, which are the chief threats to the stability of most Asian countries, and because our military presence is likely to stir up anti-American reactions and have other influences adverse to our long-range interests.

2. We should not try to induce most Asian countries to align themselves formally with us, since such alignments do not add to our security and are not likely to be as effective in giving them security as are their own unfettered nationalism and, possibly, regional groupings of like-minded countries. Far more useful, both to the security of most Asian nations and to our own, are multilateral involvements of these states with one another and with all the developed nations.

3. We should not sponsor political, social, or economic change in Asian countries, though we should be responsive to requests from them for aid in carrying out such changes, whenever we judge that these changes would help in the healthy development of these countries and that our aid could usefully contribute to this end. We run serious and unwarranted dangers when we take the initiative in sponsoring important internal changes in Asian lands or when our influence becomes so preponderant that we assume responsibility for the existence or nature of a regime. Such situations are all too likely to produce serious friction between our well-meaning efforts and their nationalism.

4. We should not seek to play the role of leader in Asia, rallying allies to our policies, but should attempt to withdraw to the role of a friendly outside supporter of individual or collective Asian initiatives. In such a role, we are more likely to be able to give effective aid to Asian countries than when we assume the leadership ourselves.

These propositions are, of course, only rough hewn, and even if they were to be accepted as fundamentally sound, we would still face the question of how to apply them. As I have said, the diversity of Asia naturally calls for many significant variations of policy. The flow of history also is not to be swiftly altered. Because of the worldwide situation at the end of the Second World War, we quite understandably and probably quite rightly assumed responsibilities in Asia and a posture in parts of that area not entirely in consonance with these propositions. They certainly are not descriptive of our present Vietnam policy. I would not advocate any sudden shift. Specifically, I do not believe that we can make any great progress toward bringing our policies in Southeast Asia in line with propositions such as these, until we have achieved a much more satisfactory solution of the Vietnam problem than is now in sight. However, unless we have guiding propositions of this type clearly in mind, we cannot take steps in the right direction when opportunity does offer, and we run the risk of wandering even further afield from them.

I have been addressing myself, of course, to the problem of our policies toward Asian countries with which we have diplomatic contacts, but some of the basic considerations also apply to Communist China. I believe that we have tended to overestimate its strength and its immediate menace to our interests and to its neighbors. The events of recent months have helped show how backward and troubled this country really is. Its economic progress will probably continue to be very slow for the foreseeable future. Thus our concern should be focused less on its immediate threat and more on its long-range development. In more specific terms, we should not concentrate so exclusively on the problem of containing Chinese aggressiveness but instead should place more emphasis on finding ways to bring the Chinese into meaningful contact with us and other nations, so that they will learn more about the realities of the outside world and will thus in time come to realize that they must accommodate themselves to these realities.

I applaud our efforts to find new contacts with the Communist Chinese through the exchange of newsmen, scholars, and other private citizens. I look upon trade contacts with Communist China as being probably of more value to the achievement of our long-range objectives than detrimental to our short-term interests. I feel that we should not oppose Peking's entry into the United Nations or other international bodies, so long as it is willing to enter on the same terms as do other countries.

Such stands would mean the clear adoption of a policy toward Communist China of "containment without isolation"—or, as the President put it last July 12, a policy of "reconciliation." I should point out, however, that I do not believe such a policy would bring any important immediate changes in our relationship with that vast country. We must continue to support the right of the people on Taiwan to self-determination and membership in the United Nations, and, that being the case, Peking may not choose to enter the United Nations for the time being. Nor does it seem probable that Communist China would respond right away to any offers from us for increased contact. However, the accumulating frustrations of the Peking regime, both in foreign policy and at home, suggest that the time may be approaching when its leaders will be forced to take more rational approaches to their international problems. It is important that, when that time comes, the Chinese realize that the doors are open for them to participate in international society and to develop closer contacts with us. In fact, the knowledge that these doors stood open might well hasten the decision in Peking to attempt to go through them.

The realization that the United States was not attempting to blackball the Peking regime in the United Nations and would welcome peaceful coexistence with Communist China would also help remove a serious psychological barrier that stands in the way of the improvement of relations between us. The Asian sensitivity toward the advanced, industrialized countries, and particularly toward the United States as the strongest of these nations, is especially marked in the case of the Chinese. China is not only the largest country in the world; for many centuries it was the most advanced, and the Chinese are certainly, and not entirely without reason, the proudest people in the world. But they have been subjected to a century and more of national humiliation at the hands of technologically superior powers. We must be especially careful to understand this historic legacy under which the Chinese labor in their relations with the outside world.

It is not surprising that the Communist Chinese fiercely resent the implication in our present policy that we have the right to pass judgment on the nature of their government and that we feel it is either unable or else unfit to continue to rule over the country that it clearly controls. The removal of these implications in our policy seems to me to be an important first step we must take if we are ever to build a more satisfactory relationship with continental

China. I might add that such a relationship is the prerequisite to a truly peaceful future for the whole Asian area.

I close with a final caution that I hope has been implicit in the foregoing remarks. There are many qualities that are demanded of us as we approach the problems of Asia—among them patience, restraint and a sensitivity to Asian views and aspirations. But most important of all, in my judgment, is a correct sense of history—and through it a truer perspective on the problems of Asia. We have failed sometimes to understand the deeply rooted historic forces at work in Asia—anticolonialism, nationalism, the eagerness to wipe out past humiliations, and the determination to advance rapidly but without losing national identity. Instead we have tended to see Asia in a historic perspective derived from other times or other places. We have, as a consequence, overreacted to images in our own minds and underreacted to the actual historical tides of Asia. Monolithic conspiracy has little future in the soil of Asia's diversity. But rapid change, even upheaval, will continue to be a part of the scene, as Asian countries seek to close the gap between themselves and the advanced nations. We must learn to take such upheavals in stride, putting aside cold war demonology and using our influence with caution and restraint to help channel these changes toward constructive ends.

These are a few thoughts I have on our Asian policies, presented in bald and oversimplified form. I do not offer them as carefully formulated policy statements, but as concepts that may help stimulate the Committee in its thinking about these problems.

PLANS COMMENSURATE WITH NEEDS

THE CRISIS OF THE CITIES:
THE DANGER OF THE GHETTO [1]

WHITNEY M. YOUNG, JR. [2]

The urban crisis may be viewed from many angles. The architect sees in some of the new buildings monuments to ugliness. The city planner—the discriminating one, that is—deplores the hopeless congestion of the streets and arterial highways. The scientist looks at the leaden sky and cries "Pollutants." Doubtless everyone is sensitive to the poverty, the slums, the racial tensions, and the social deterioration in the major centers. The crisis is each of these problems, and it is all of them, and many more. Despite the movement from the rural areas to the cities—as well as because of it—and despite the attraction of the big place for economic and social reasons, the large cities are in deep trouble. As United States Commissioner of Education Harold Howe II said recently, Plutarch was right in calling the city a teacher, with its many facets of art, commerce, entertainment, and the like offering their own lessons. "But the kind of lesson you learn depends on where in the classroom you sit."

Urban trouble is a challenge to our social structure. There is despair on our streets, and it cries out for sympathetic, statesmanlike resolution.

We have not suffered from a dearth of rhetoric on the plight of the cities. But few speakers have come so closely to grips with the core difficulties as did Whitney M. Young, Jr., in his wide-ranging address at Cambridge, Massachusetts, on February 28, 1967, before a meeting of the Joint Center for Urban Studies of the Massachusetts Institute of Technology and Harvard University. Mr. Young opened his talk with a statement of his central idea—a technique often discussed in our textbooks on public speaking:

> Here at the outset I may as well state my central thesis, which is that the central cities of this increasingly urban nation are not only threatened with collapse, but are, in fact, collapsing, in large part due to the fiscal drain of the ghetto. As a consequence, what we are confronted with in the civil rights struggle is no longer a problem for the Negro alone, but for the whole society.

[1] Joint Center for Urban Studies of the Massachusetts Institute of Technology and Harvard University, Cambridge, Massachusetts, February 28, 1967. Text furnished by Catherine C. Hemenway, Assistant Director of Public Relations, National Urban League, Inc., with permission for this reprint.

[2] For biographical note, see Appendix.

With detailed analysis, Mr. Young, who since 1961 has been the Executive Director of the National Urban League, which incidentally found jobs for some fifty thousand Negroes last year, outlined the nature and dimension of the slum problem. He pointed to efforts to deal with the problem—some of them quite successful. However, he underscored the massive undertakings urgently needed if our cities are not "to become centers of chaos." Finally, he reiterated the theme of his speech:

> It is obvious that the urban crisis stems in large part from the failure to resolve the problems that confront the Negro and it is obvious what the Negro wants. He wants what white Americans are able to take for granted. He wants the same opportunity to earn a living, the same freedom of choice in the selection of housing and the same quality of education for his children. He wants dignity as well as opportunity, performance on the part of white Americans as well as pledge.

Time's essay of October 28, 1966, ended on this note: "The job of helping [the Negro] to meet his legitimate needs may well continue to be the nation's most urgent piece of domestic business for decades to come." There is reason—understandable reason—why he may not be willing to wait decades.

Students of public speaking interested in further reflections on the ghetto and the plight of minority citizens will find these additional speeches rewarding: Secretary Robert C. Weaver's address in Philadelphia on August 1, 1966; and Senator Robert F. Kennedy's three talks on programs for the urban crisis: January 20, 21, and 22, 1966.

Here at the outset I may as well state my central thesis, which is that the central cities of this increasingly urban nation are not only threatened with collapse but are, in fact, collapsing, in large part due to the fiscal drain of the ghetto. As a consequence, what we are confronted with in the civil rights struggle is no longer a problem for the Negro alone, but for the whole society.

Throughout the country, the major cities are in trouble, scarred by slums and ghettos, threatened by racial strife and crippled by inadequate finances. Predictions are that the nation's urban population will double by the beginning of the next century and unless adequate steps are taken to avoid disaster, so will the problems of the big cities. Without radical action, our cities are destined to become centers of chaos.

One speaks of the possibility of violence with caution. Too often, to predict the possibility of violence is interpreted as an incitement to violence. But I infinitely prefer to be called an alarmist than to stand by, a silent witness to impending crisis. If what I say is interpreted as the message of an alarmist, then I can only say that Paul Revere was an alarmist.

I assume that what we are really talking about here, in talking about the crisis of the cities, are the problems of people—that we are not confining ourselves simply to questions of bricks and mortar in our consideration of the urban scene—and that we are concerned with the problems of people living in an urban environment, an environment to which mankind did not come naturally. Many of these problems derive from tangible factors, many from intangibles —from feelings of anonymity, of being nameless and faceless, a feeling of being lost in the great urban mass. Most of these latter derive from rootlessness and the lack of a personal stake in the community.

The questions before us become questions of how to provide the urban resident, and most particularly the slum and ghetto resident, with a stake in his own community, how to diminish the sense of anonymity he feels, how to reduce the impersonality of the urban environment, and, in the process, how to approach all the problems affecting the society-at-large.

Urbanization, first of all, causes severe stresses both for the community and the individual. Housing shortages are chronic in all our major cities. Educational facilities in our slums are inferior from the standpoint of social and welfare services. Urbanization perhaps has its most profound impact on the structure of family institutions. The old traditions and values of the original family unit disintegrate under the impact of urbanization. The problems of the ghetto invade every aspect of life. It is our responsibility, in this society, to insure that the same skills, genius and creative drive that have gone into brick-and-mortar progress throughout the world, into the building of bridges, highways and tunnels, and indeed into smashing the atom and flights into space, must and do, now, go into planning with people for their own social needs. Only in this way can our cities reflect viable functional modes of productive living rather than struggles for survival against despair, hopelessness and frustration. Children then are not walled off from grass and sky and adults need not be faced with a monotonous routine which, at best, becomes a matter of existing—and without much choice.

Man in the urban complex has more than just physiological needs—the needs for food, clothing and shelter. He also has psychological needs—the needs for attention, affection, status and a feeling of making a contribution to his community.

At one time a man was adequate and had status if he simply provided a roof over the head of his family and could give his children a piece of candy from time to time. To be able to perform these simple acts was sufficient to obtain physiological and psychological satisfaction and to provide him with status in the community where he lived.

But living in the city demands more in terms of skills and of sophistication and so, man, newly transplanted within the urban complex, faces, and feels, alienation, a sense of rejection and loneliness, which makes even more painful the vision of those who are more affluent than he in the affluent society he sees all about him; and he either reacts with hostility by concluding that he is being exploited by the forces that are making others affluent, or he is diminished in his own self-estimation and says to himself, "I'm a failure." Such self-devaluation carries over into his role as a husband and as a father and into his concept of his own status and dignity.

Under the burden of anxiety, individual urban man becomes apathetic, overwhelmed, withdrawn. Because he doesn't want to acknowledge that he himself is inadequate in a new setting, he must cite powers bigger than himself, and what he says to himself and the community is, "I don't care," "I don't want to succeed anyhow," "You can't beat the system," "You can't fight City Hall." Apathy is hopelessness, powerlessness and the forgetting of the most important fact, the fact that money is not power, that status is not power, that color can never be power. That the greatest power is to be right. And if you're right and believe in that right, you can get power. The Negro cause in America today is right and that's why it upsets those who refuse to accept change.

The question before us is how, given all the factors that make up reality, we can build into urban society the human institutions which will provide the experience of community. The problem is how to make the urban environment human and humane, how to make the geographical entity in which so many people reside livable, how to guarantee that people do not live as part of an amorphous mass, as impersonal cogs in the urban complex where the size and formality and the impersonal quality of the urban setting tend to deprive the individual man of his sense of identity.

I am prepared to say without hesitation that, in large measure, this country's success or failure will be gauged by the success or failure of Negro Americans in their struggle for existence in the urban environment, and on the success or failure of white Americans in meeting the challenges posed by the circumstances in which the bulk of American Negroes live. The real test of the urban structure will be whether or not the Negro within it benefits and succeeds on a par with his white peer in the larger society.

The simple fact is that despite all the frenzied activity, despite all the well intentioned efforts, and all the signs of real progress in the last decade and more, the gap between nonwhite citizens in the United States and white citizens has not been closed. In most instances it is not even narrowing—it is widening.

The time is clearly past for halfway measures, token gestures, pilot programs and halfhearted, one-dimensional, small-scale efforts, no matter how well intentioned. The crisis of our cities defies any such simple solutions. The expanding ghettos are not only thoroughly destructive to the people who live in them, but they threaten the welfare of every major city with strangulation and dry-rot. As one mark of our urbanity today we now have more people living in slums than we have on farms. The United States

Census shows 21 million on farms; 22 million in slums—and that was in 1960. There is little doubt but that current figures, if available as of today, would show a still more remarkable picture.

We are using a slingshot for a job that calls for nuclear weapons. We are applying band-aids in the curious expectation of stopping the growth of an advanced cancer.

Three things are obvious. First, it is obvious that, whatever specific approach to the problems of the cities, the job is too big for government alone. Success will require the fullest possible commitment from every segment of this society, from the private sector as well as the public sector, from industry, labor, Federal, state and local government, as well as from the nonprofit sector as represented by the foundations.

Second, we cannot confine ourselves to any single approach, or to any one method. There must be concerted and coordinated action on many fronts at once, in education, in housing, in employment and in health and welfare. The job requires the full application of American genius and imagination.

It is also essential to realize that the debate now raging over whether to disperse the ghetto or to rebuild it is a debate without substance. Housing stock in the ghetto must be redeemed or replaced no matter who lives there—this year or next. The schools in the ghetto must be made excellent no matter who attends them —this year or next. And neither can wait on solutions to other problems before the beginnings are made there.

Third, it is obvious that within the Federal sector, with many of the legislative battles now won, that the struggle in the immediate future will lie to a considerable extent in the struggle for appropriations massive enough to get the job done that must be done.

The overriding question is one of the *will* to achieve definitive solutions. The first imperative is that we devise programs appropriately scaled to the size and urgency of the problems we face.

Recently, we have seen a growing recognition of the need for a massive effort, as expressed in the "Freedom Budget," which calls for an expenditure of $185 billion over the next ten years to be de-

rived from the nation's "economic growth dividend"—a plan which
fleshes out, puts meat on the bones of the domestic Marshall Plan
we in the Urban League enunciated several years ago. We support
this, and other, proposals which actively serve the same ends. These
are proposals properly scaled to the size and urgency of the urban
problems we face. Only when the need is understood on this scale
and long-range programing is undertaken along these lines, will
we be able to assume that we are on the road to adequate solutions.

Nothing short of action on the scale indicated in the "Freedom
Budget" will allow us to rescue the cities from the problems that
now beset them, restore a viable tax base to major municipalities,
create a full-employment economy, and provide every American
with a decent home and a decent education, all of which are essential objectives if the crisis of the cities is to be overcome. Otherwise we will have to face all the implications of finding our central
cities more and more fully occupied by a dispossessed, undereduc-
cated, underemployed, embittered, angry, impatient, low-income
population.

New York City is a good case in point. What is happening in
one degree or another in every major metropolitan area in the
country. New York's annual budget crisis occurs with the regu-
larity of clockwork. It did not begin with the Lindsay administration and it will not end with the Lindsay administration. Where
it will end may well determine the fate of the Republic.

A year ago, New York, deep in its desperate annual search for
funds to make up the difference between public revenues and the
cost of essential public services, faced a budget deficit of $518 mil-
lion. The Mayor stated then "that without new revenues a major
reduction of *all* city services will be necessary resulting in a drastic
change in the quality of life in New York City." In the course of
the crisis the New York Stock Exchange threatened to leave the
city; the City University was threatened with seriously cutting
back on the number of students it could accept and city hospitals
were threatened with a catastrophic mass resignation of nurses for
want of adequate pay and for a time municipal hospital doors were

closed to all but emergency patients. New taxes were enacted and the city survived.

Today one year later, of course, the city is in the grips of this year's budget crisis and the Mayor has stated that "New York City is at a crossroads. We must find the revenues to keep city government financially viable or so cut back services that government provides that the city becomes less and less livable."

The New York Stock Exchange still has not resolved the question of where to settle, and this month Pepsico, the American Can Company, Corn Products, Flintcote, and Olin-Mathieson have announced that they will move their operations out of the city. More disturbing, Leonard C. Yaseen, board chairman of the Fantus Company, the world's largest location consultants, has said that "six years ago we might have done six relocation studies in an entire year, but in 1967 we may conduct forty such studies."

This is the kind of disruption of the normal business and civic cycle that American cities are experiencing now in the present moment and it is symptomatic of the price we as a nation are paying for our failure to resolve the problems of the ghetto.

Put another way, HHFA [Housing and Home Finance Agency] figures show that the average cost per citizen for municipal services in a blighted area is $7 but the area pays back only $4.25; whereas in a good area, the average cost of essential services is $3.60 per citizen and the area pays back $11.30. Because of the distressed conditions under which they live, the number of Negroes on the public welfare rolls is increasing and one third of the $3.5 billion we spend today as a nation for public aid, education and housing goes to Negroes who constitute only 11 per cent of the population. In light of these facts, the fiscal management of the cities becomes increasingly difficult and the plight of the ghetto resident becomes increasingly acute.

It is inconceivable to me that responsible legislators and leaders in industry and commerce should any longer deny strong support to all measures necessary to correct the evils that pervade ghetto life and drain the resources of American cities.

And yet, what, for instance, is the picture in Washington today, and what is the picture in the private sector? In both arenas, it is exceedingly mixed. In Washington, leadership in the Executive branch is strong. You can give Johnson hell if you like on Vietnam, but the commitment of the Executive to solutions to our number one domestic problem is beyond doubt. Added evidence accumulates every day. To talk to people at the policy-making levels in the Executive departments is often immensely rewarding. The best of them are creative, sophisticated in the nature of the problem, passionately committed to solutions and imaginative in the use of legislative tools already at hand.

The picture in the Congress is, in large part, another story altogether and this is not just a result of the elections in November. The elections in November only serve to make matters worse. They can't be said to have been all that good prior to November.

For one thing the pace of implementation of domestic legislation is dependent upon manipulation of the fiscal machinery of government. Much worthy legislation languishes for lack of adequate appropriations. The Model Cities legislation enacted by the last Congress, for example, is conceived to put the full resources of the nation—Federal, state and municipal, public and private—to work to achieve not only the physical, but the social, rehabilitation of the cities. To date, the total sum appropriated for Model Cities is $11 million and that is for planning. No monies have yet been appropriated for the implementation of the Model Cities legislation.

Moreover, it is interesting to ponder the fact that this appropriation is in the control of a subcommittee of the House Appropriations Committee which is composed of ten men, not one of whom comes from a major city. The chairman, Representative Joe L. Evins, is from Smithville, Tennessee, a town with a population of 2,348. The largest city represented on this committee is Springfield, Massachusetts, with a population of 174,463. Other members of the committee come from towns of 8,780; 2,428; and 5,699.

To the President's full credit, his budget message recommended appropriations for the implementation of the Model Cities legislation at the full level of departmental request. What the appropriations subcommittee will choose, in its wisdom, to recommend is anybody's guess.

A further part of the problem in the Congress is that, in general, the northern liberal representative in the Congress, the man who votes "right" on issues affecting the Negro, is neither as shrewd nor as committed to his objectives as the southern representative. In practice, the northern liberal tends to be completely outmaneuvered by the committed southerner and the key to effective implementation of legislation is inevitably tied to the Federal purse strings which are firmly in the grip of the Congress.

Quite aside from the deliberations of the ten small-town men who, by virtue of their seniority, sit astride the appropriations for Model Cities, I greatly fear what the record of some members of northern congressional delegations, for example, may be when they are called upon to vote on massive appropriation rather than on, say, the Civil Rights Bill of 1967. Many a northern congressman, whose heart isn't really in it, may find it thoroughly feasible to vote against an appropriations bill, which is poorly understood by his constituency, whereas he could never vote against a civil rights bill. As we enter into a new phase of the struggle, where appropriations massive enough to do the job under existing legislation are of the essence, the lack of commitment among many northern congressmen becomes a matter for serious concern.

It is further interesting to note that, at a time when it has become clear that dispersal of the ghetto is essential to the health of the central cities, that it was a congressman from New York City who required inclusion of language in the Model Cities bill which precludes use of the Model Cities program to effect dispersal of the ghetto. In the same vein, more than a decade after the Supreme Court decision desegregating the schools, the Elementary and Secondary Education Act was passed, but only after language was inserted which states that "desegregation shall not mean assignment to public schools in order to overcome racial imbalance."

The picture in the private sector is no less interesting. Hundreds of companies have voluntarily complied with the President's Plans for Progress, and many have proved imaginative and inventive in dealing with the problems of recruiting, training and motivating minority workers. But the job and the responsibility of the private sector does not stop there.

I like to cite the situation as it now exists in Hartford, Connecticut, where, I am informed, the most progressive element in the community is the Chamber of Commerce, and the most regressive elements are the two major political parties, the Democratic the more so in that it is the stronger. Now the reason for the progressivism of the Chamber of Commerce, I am told, is that being good Yankee businessmen, its members take the position that they don't care what color people are, they are concerned only with getting them back on the tax rolls. "If you have to educate them, educate them," these men say. "If you have to build them houses, build them houses. But let's get them back on the tax rolls." This is my idea of an enlightened outlook for business and businessmen, and I hope and pray that the business community generally rapidly accepts the wisdom of this approach—both for the welfare of the Negro community and for the sake of the future of the cities.

There are further encouraging signs on the horizon. Within the recent past, for example, the New York Board of Trade, which is a major business-civic organization in New York, has taken the position that it is deeply aware of the total environment in which business operates and that equal concern must be given in management's planning for environmental factors other than the purely economic. The Board of Trade has determined to take an active part in identifying management's rightful role in the solution of socioeconomic problems besetting New York City, including those of the ghetto. There are even rumblings from within the National Association of Manufacturers emanating from a deep urge to image-changing through a new examination of the role of the corporate structure in relation to the socioeconomic problems that haunt the entire society.

As the pressures of the urban crisis continue to mount, it is possible that the most significant pressures for change will come not from their accustomed sources but from a concerned, aware and affected private sector. It is also possible that the Model Cities program which requires the active cooperation of the private sector will effect the first happy marriage in the solution of the problems besetting urban areas between Federal, state and local government and private interests.

To revert now to the coming struggle for massive appropriations as opposed to new legislation at the Federal level. The need, of course, varies from area to area. In general, the necessary legislative tools already exist for a broadscale attack on the problems of housing and manpower training.

The Department of Housing and Urban Development has a battery of techniques available to it, prime among which are the Turnkey Housing formula for the rehabilitation and replacement of substandard housing stock, and the leasing program which makes it possible for local Public Housing Authorities to lease apartments at will for use as public housing units. Massive application of the Turnkey concept alone could serve to eradicate substandard housing, estimated at 5 million units nationally, within the next ten years, if a massive effort were undertaken, as indeed it must be.

In addition, HUD has the tools at hand to create broad opportunities for home ownership by low-income people, a proposition the Urban League stresses as essential to any plan for the physical and social redemption of the ghetto. Home ownership, and the pride of ownership, constitute the surest way to create a stake in the community for individual families and to guarantee the health and stability of the community over the long haul.

The Urban League has proposed that leases on all rehabilitated housing made available to low-income families be combined with an option to buy, either on a cooperative or a condominium basis. Under this proposal, as a family's income increases, the family could undertake purchase rather than being required to move. Present housing law contains a provision for private ownership of public housing in attached and semidetached houses, a device so far being utilized only in St. Louis.

We have also proposed that private ownership of low-cost housing be further encouraged through the introduction of a federally

subsidized below-market interest rate of not more than 3 per cent
for the purchase of rehabilitated substandard housing by low-income families, a precedent for which currently exists in the Model
Cities Act, which authorizes the purchase of such mortgages by the
Federal National Mortgage Association under its special assistance
program. In this connection, we would further urge the extension
of such a below-market interest rate to all returning veterans.

Thirdly, we have proposed that one component in any program
for the mass rehabilitation of slum housing be a provision whereby
slum residents can obtain a "sweat equity" in ownership, through
contributing physical labor to the rehabilitation and construction
process, and that this provision for "sweat equity" be coupled with
on-the-job-training in the construction trades. A precedent for
"sweat equity" in low-cost housing exists in HUD's Mutual Help
Program which so far has been applied on only a limited basis, and
never yet in an urban setting.

It is not my purpose to discuss these proposals at length here.
The point I wish to make is that in the field of housing the question
now is largely one of the imaginative and, most importantly, the
massive use of presently available housing tools. What must be
developed within existing legislation is a basic framework for action
consisting of the fullest possible use of the credit and subsidy powers
of the Federal Government on a massive and coordinated basis and
in a fashion designed to involve the initiative and incentives of
competitive free enterprise.

Again, the debate about whether to "gild" the ghetto or disperse
it is irrelevant. The housing stock in the ghetto has to be redeemed
or replaced *now* no matter who is to live there now or at a later date.

As in housing, the laws on the books affecting manpower training are generally adequate. Programs have been written to cover
most contingencies in this field and there is adequate leeway for
experiment. What is essential, again, is that these tools be utilized
on a scale commensurate with the problem, with the need to train
all those who need training in order to become gainfully employed.

In both education and welfare there is a continuing need for
legislation if, on the one hand, quality and integration are indeed

to become the hallmarks of our public school system, and if, on the other, poverty is to be eradicated in this affluent society.

It is still very early to tell what the results to date have been of Title I of the Elementary and Secondary Education Act in contributing either to the quality of education in the schools or to the integration of the schools. Present indications are that while some schools have been able to make very good use of the monies provided by this Act, many schools were unprepared to utilize the monies to full advantage and, in the eyes of concerned people, they have often resulted in what could be called "add-on" programs, programs which have just provided the schools with more of the same old uninspired and uninspiring materials, equipment and program they have had before.

As for the progress of integration, the United States Civil Rights Commission has just reported that thirteen years after the Supreme Court decision desegregating the schools, 75 per cent of all Negro children and 83 per cent of all white children still go to schools that are 90 per cent or more segregated, whether the segregation be of Negro children or of white; that the achievement levels of Negro children have been only slightly affected by so-called "compensatory programs" in these segregated schools; and that they will continue to suffer academically unless legislation is enacted that requires racial balance in all the nation's public schools. Like the Supreme Court decision of 1954, the current report by the Civil Rights Commission holds that both Negro and white children suffer when isolated from the mainstream of society. It further states that even though state and local governments in the North do not decree segregated school systems, Negroes are nevertheless denied equal protection of the law through a subtle combination of assignment patterns, school board decisions and the selection of school sites, which affect them quite as severely as those practices which have permeated the South.

The problem, obviously, of desegregating the schools is not an easy one. No schoolman wants to turn his whole system inside out in order to desegregate, but, often, that's the only real solution. Some inspired efforts have been undertaken in cities and towns across the country including Xenia, Ohio, where white support was enlisted for desegregation with a demonstration school in the Negro neighborhood; in Irondequoit, New York, where Negro youngsters were successfully imported into the school system of an all-white community; in Evanston, Illinois, where a computer was used to redistrict school attendance areas and to redistribute white and Negro students in combination with a dynamic education improvement program for the whole district; in York, Pennsylvania, where Negro youngsters were gradually slipped into elementary schools, grade by grade, starting with kindergarten in combination with a human relations program for students, parents and teachers; in Teaneck, New Jersey, where developing *de facto* segregation was rooted out by converting an elementary school into a central school for all sixth-graders; and in Riverside, California, where a crisis situation paved the way for integration of the schools.

In Riverside, where schoolmen were committed to the concept of the neighborhood school, someone else in the community wasn't. So, he burned one of them down. With a Molotov cocktail. At midnight.

A crisis? Yes—and an opportunity, too, as it turned out. The school's destruction forced immediate integration of its students into other schools. And this integration went off so smoothly that, within a matter of months, the Riverside Superintendent of Schools was able to schedule integration of the city's remaining racially imbalanced schools and predict that "minority pupils will be as well received by staff members and other pupils as those who were integrated as a result of the fire."

Which is not to say that this school superintendent or any other sane schoolman recommends school burning as a desegregation catalyst. But the fact remains that, in this case, the fire stimulated fast and effective action. Within a month of the fire, Riverside's administration was able to announce a solid plan to desegregate totally within two years.

Or—consider the education plaza, or educational park, as it's being developed in Orange, New Jersey. The concept is simple enough. If small neighborhood grade schools are creating a *de facto* segregation problem, and the entire K-12 system is getting out of date to boot, the idea is to close the schools and consolidate. The first step toward an education plaza has already been taken in East Orange. A pilot group of 250 fifth- and sixth-graders is being introduced to nongraded, individualized instructional techniques which will be used in the projected school plant. Land purchase and construction of a $1.5 million base building is scheduled for completion in 1968. A large intermediate school, an upper school and a lower school, are scheduled to follow in that order. The base building will be used for new teaching programs for the plaza and will be integrated into that structure later. Total implementation time for the plaza, which will also include a resource tower and junior college, a "lively arts" center, gymnasiums, a covered stadium and a large parking lot—is pegged at fifteen years.

It has even been suggested that one way to desegregate the schools is to strip the ghetto of schools for a period of time. The rationale behind this suggestion is that given a situation where you have an all-black school here and an all-white school there and perhaps an integrated school in between, the logical movement of pupils would be from the all-black school to the all-white school, and vice versa, but that, in fact, this two-way movement doesn't work. You can get movement from the all-black school to the all-white school, but you can't get comparable movement from the all-white school to the all-black school as long as the latter is perceived by the white community as an all-Negro school. Hence the proposal is to strip the ghetto of schools by moving the student population out and leaving the buildings empty if need be until such time as the school in question is no longer perceived as an all-Negro school; at that time it can be reopened with an enriched curriculum designed to attract white students as well as black on the magnet theory. I am by no means facetious in seriously urging that this approach be explored fully where everything else seems to fail.

To be good, the schools of this nation have to be desegregated. Where the will to desegregate exists, the schools are being desegregated.

There are still other things that a given school district can do. The middle-school concept, or the 4-4-4 system can change perceptions of the all-Negro school so that schools attract a more representative student body. Shuttle lines can be established, so that kids can get to an integrated school in a ten-minute bus ride. Bussing, like the idea of Federal control of the schools, is a false issue. White parents, who can afford to, have been bussing their children to private schools for generations. The rural consolidated school has depended on bussing for decades. And as far as Federal control is concerned, out of the total spent on education in this country for education at all levels, including higher education, only 8 per cent comes from Federal sources. At the elementary and secondary levels, the percentage is a mere 4 per cent.

The legislative route to achieving integration of the schools might result from a happy marriage between certain provisions of bills introduced in the last session of the Congress by Senator Edward Kennedy and Representative Adam Clayton Powell. The Kennedy bill would amend Title IV of the Civil Rights Act of 1964 to authorize the Commissioner of Education to provide technical assistance and grants to school boards which have drawn up programs for overcoming racial imbalance in their public schools. In other words, it would provide monies, which present legislation does *not* do, to meet the costs of desegregation. There are no coercive provisions in this bill whatsoever. The Powell bill, on the contrary, provides that every school district shall report to the United States Commissioner of Education on the racial composition of its student population by building and if, by 1970, any building exceeds the minority population of the school district by more than 20 per cent, it would get no more Federal money. For instance, in New York City, where the minority public school population throughout the City is 33 per cent of the total, any school with a minority population of 54 per cent as of 1970 would be deprived of any further Federal aid. Solutions are possible. It is not beyond the genius of America to find solutions.

The major needs for welfare legislation are threefold. One most important step is legislation requiring that by a given date, the states pay in full their own standards of assistance, which at this point, numbers of them do not. Further legislation is required in order to establish a major training component for people now receiving Aid for Dependent Children plus incentives to work. At present, we give the needy income. And we take away most of that income if the recipient gets the smallest job, causing needless waste and demoralization. Worse still, public assistance as presently written and administered encourages the disintegration of the family. In most states, the main assistance program, Aid for Dependent Children, is not available if there is an able-bodied man in the house, even if he is not working. All too often it is necessary for the father to leave his children so that they can eat. It is bad enough to provide incentives for idleness but even worse to provide legislative incentives for desertion.

Perhaps the best solution would be for the Federal Government to assume the cost of providing a minimum income. Nothing is quite so certain to provide an antidote for poverty as the provision of definite and dependable income. Ideally, such income would derive from expanded job opportunities, including jobs on needed public works, but in the absence of sufficient job opportunities, a minimum income is eminently desirable.

Numerous arguments are raised against this solution, the foremost among which is the assertion that it would destroy individual incentive. Yet, nothing is more certain than that we now have a welfare system that could not be better designed to destroy incentives if it had been planned for that specific purpose.

Perhaps the best solution to the crisis of the cities would be for the Federal Government to assume the cost of providing a minimum income, and thus freeing the cities from the present burden of welfare costs. In the years of the farm crisis, Federal Government did this for agriculture. In these years of urban crisis, we need a system that directs funds not by some formula to the country at large, but to the points of greatest need, in short, to the large cities. The United States Conference of Mayors, for one, is convinced that the cities are being shortchanged in a period when their own taxing resources are manifestly too limited to halt urban decay.

To transfer income maintenance to the Federal Government, would be to free big city budgets of a large share of their welfare payments and would be an enormous step in the right direction, leaving the cities free to meet problems which can be met only on local terms.

Whatever the analysis of our urban problems, whatever combination of approaches are taken toward their solution, one point is clear and that is that there is no simple way. The problems that confront us are desperate problems, infinite in their complexity and interrelatedness, and we must use every tool in the social arsenal to achieve solutions.

As one additional tool, which requires no legislative action, just administrative decision in both the public and private sectors, I would draw your attention to the Urban League's proposal for Operation Urban Survival, first enunciated at our annual Conference in Philadelphia last August and predicated on the following facts.

The explosive increase of the Negro population in northern, central and western cities represents one of the most dramatic social changes in urban history. No other ethnic group has ever made up as large a proportion of the population as does the Negro today. In 1910, when the Urban League was founded, 73 per cent of all Negroes lived in rural areas. Today, 73 per cent of all Negroes live in cities. In just one decade, New York City lost a middle-class white population almost the size of Washington, D.C., and gained a nonwhite population almost the size of Pittsburgh.

The United States Civil Rights Commission has reported that if all of New York City were as jammed with people as several of the worst blocks in Harlem, the entire population of the United States could fit into three of the City's five boroughs, with two left over for expansion.

By 1970, it is estimated that there will be 18 million Negroes living in our urban centers and before long, ten of the major cities of the United States will be more than 50 per cent Negro. Washington, D.C. already is and has been for nearly a decade. Newark, which was 34.4 per cent Negro at the time of the 1960 census, is now over 50 per cent Negro.

In Detroit, Baltimore, Cleveland and St. Louis, Negroes constitute a third or more of the population and in Chicago, Philadelphia, Cincinnati, Indianapolis and Oakland, they constitute more than one fourth of the population. The impact of the expanding ghetto is being felt in smaller cities like New Haven and Gary, San Diego, Buffalo and Rochester, Toledo and Akron, Fort Wayne and Milwaukee, Kansas City and Wichita. Not even the South is immune. New Orleans is 41 per cent Negro, Memphis and Atlanta, 38 per cent.

Whether you accept or reject the basic immorality inherent in the existence and growth of the racial ghetto, it is clear that the emerging picture in the central cities has implications which overshadow past social and economic revolutions and make them pale into insignificance. As long as the ghettos continue to swell, the welfare of American cities is in jeopardy.

The welfare of the American city depends upon the stability of its fiscal base; its ability to finance those collective necessities which make it possible for large numbers of people to live close together, allow commerce to thrive and create those public facilities and services which make urban life tolerable. Blighted areas—and all the ghettos of our major cities are blighted—work intolerable hardships on the people who live in them and drain the total community of its financial resources. Such areas are utterly unable to make a satisfactory contribution to the city treasury in return for services. Taxable income diminishes as the ghettos expand and the cost of public services mushrooms. This is the vise in which most of our major cities are caught.

In light of these facts, the Urban League's Operation Urban Survival represents a major additional measure for the alleviation of these conditions.

Operation Urban Survival calls, quite simply, for public and private institutional building in the ghetto, for a nationwide program of locating new commercial, governmental, industrial, cultural and educational buildings and developments in slum areas in order to spearhead the transformation of the ghettos into viable, integrated communities. *Where* such facilities are located can have as much social meaning as the purposes they are intended to house and social costs to the community can be vastly reduced by just such enlightened measures as this.

Widely implemented, Operation Urban Survival would mean a vast upgrading of ghetto areas. Just as location of the United Nations upgraded a blighted area of the East Side of New York, just as location of Lincoln Center upgraded a blighted area of the West Side, and just as Rockefeller Center upgraded a deteriorating section of midtown Manhattan, the location of major commercial, governmental, cultural and educational institutions designed to service the total community, black and white, in the ghetto, would not only upgrade blighted areas but would have a multitude of tangential, and eminently desirable, effects.

This proposal addresses itself to the social, commercial, civic and cultural vitality of areas now alienated from the larger community. A major, though intangible, side effect would be the improvement of communications between the races, an essential to progress which is largely lacking at present.

Operation Urban Survival means creating jobs within the ghetto that will command a mixed working population and is conceived in the belief that a mixed working population will lead to a mixed residential population. Dispersal of the ghetto, essential to the health of the central cities, requires not only that Negroes move out of the ghetto but that whites have good reason to move in.

In one stroke, Operation Urban Survival can bring new life and vitality to a decaying part of the city. It will generate new hope in the slums as adults find jobs and youngsters see that education can lead to tangible results. It will generate many kinds of peripheral enterprise and development, further adding to the vitality of the community. Such projects in the hearts of the ghettos will provide visible evidence that the city cares, that neglect and abuse are at an end, and that integration is a living force in city life. Most important of all, it will end the isolation of the ghetto from the rest of the community and is essential to achieving healthy traffic in both directions.

For example, if the two million square feet now planned for consolidation of New York State Office space in the World Trade Center on a site in downtown Manhattan, were consolidated instead in Harlem, we would have a facility in the Harlem community that would meet all the standards of Operation Urban Survival. It would employ a mixed working population, it would establish a healthy in-and-out traffic in the area, it would lead to the development of peripheral enterprise and would create a standing reservoir of jobs in the ghetto, and it could be expected to lead to a mixed residential pattern.

In addition, it is more than probable that construction of the two million square feet of office space now scheduled for the World Trade Center downtown would prove significantly cheaper to build in Harlem.

There is every reason for state and municipal governments to respond favorably to this proposal inasmuch as substantial portions of their funds go to bridge the gap caused by the economic conditions of the ghettos. The private sector has a comparable stake in this means to establishing the future fiscal health of the cities.

In conclusion, it is obvious that the urban crisis stems in large part from the failure to resolve the problems that confront the Negro and it is obvious what the Negro wants. He wants what white Americans are able to take for granted. He wants the same opportunity to earn a living, the same freedom of choice in the selection of housing and the same quality of education for his children. He wants dignity as well as opportunity, performance on the part of white Americans as well as pledge.

If there is no genuine conviction about the rightness of integration and human relations and no will to arrive at solutions—then laws alone cannot solve the problem—and the future welfare of our cities is in serious jeopardy.

I hope I have made it utterly clear that nothing less than massive effort will produce significant results. We must marshal all our available resources for the job at hand and proceed on a scale commensurate with the task. We are in terrible danger, and our cities in desperate peril, if any among us permit ourselves the luxury of "thinking small."

PROFESSIONAL INSIGHTS

ACCELERATION OR DIRECTION? [1]

LOUIS T. BENEZET [2]

Those of us who were teaching during the 1930's can recall with pleasant memory the intellectual ferment that bubbled excitedly in many of the large colleges and universities across the land. Twenty years later, professors were complaining about the seeming passivity, even apathy, of their students. Today the sound of protest is mightily in the air, but with different overtones. Whereas in the 1930's a student group might object spiritedly to a specific policy—compulsory ROTC, for example—today the protest is more likely to be directed not only at an alleged evil but also at large—against a system, against this amorphous something called the Establishment. In an existentialist context, perhaps, the students are in revolt, as Irving Kristol observed, "not so much because things are bad for them or for others, but because things are what they are for them and for others." This is not to condemn responsible dissent. Many would agree with Samuel Gould, president of the State University of New York, that excellence will be hard to get "if everyone is expected to think as everyone else does, to act as everyone else does, and never to challenge anyone or anything." In his speech "The University as a Catalyst for Change," delivered on November 1, 1965, Dr. Gould remarked:

> Show me the university or, indeed, the community where no unpopular idea can find opportunity for utterance, where the status quo can never be challenged, and I will show you a place of sterility and inaction, of self-satisfaction bordering on the reactionary. Show me the organization where everyone must conform in order to advance or even survive, and I will show you a place where excellence in its true meaning has been sublimated to a condition of mediocrity.

The battle—if it may be so unhappily labeled—does, however, involve the faculty and students as active parties in dispute. And the literature on the breach of feelings is rather extensive. Recently, Dean Paul A. Varg of Michigan State University indicated that our institutions of higher learning "threaten to become houses divided":

> The purely intellectual commitment appears sterile to students and it is always suspected of camouflaging apathy. The noisy demon-

[1] National Conference of Academic Deans, Los Angeles, California, January 16, 1967. Text furnished by Dr. Benezet, with permission for this reprint.

[2] For biographical note, see Appendix.

stration, on the other hand, may appear to the senior members of the academic community as an attempt to feel self-important. This house divided may be nothing more than evidence that, in the words of Matthew Arnold, we live between two worlds, "one dead, the other powerless to be born."

Dr. Louis T. Benezet, whose address is reprinted below, opened his remarks with a reference to "the war between students and teachers"—a war of which neither group seemed fully aware. The conflict is, however, an old one. But over the years student activism, especially of the political variety, has been closely identified more with institutions in Western Europe and Latin America than with those in the United States. I remember well a young man from South America in one of my classes some twenty years ago expressing an unbelieving amazement not unmixed with horror at the triflingly indirect part that our students played in the political life of the country. Were he to assess the students' role today, he would doubtless note a measurable change.

Dr. Benezet's address deals in a distinctive manner with the cleavage between students and teacher-administrators:

> The motion of our academic carrousel is accelerating. Part of the acceleration is due to the driven energies of the people on board. As students clamor for freedoms from the administration, presidents and deans plead harder for professors to draw nigher to students and calm them down. As professors translate such appeals into their language of additional academic requirements, the students accept the additional charge but then press for unbridled indulgences in their remaining hours free from study. There are dynamics enough in the carrousel to make it spin faster as a result of its own workings.

Eventually "the attritions of a society characterized by velocity rather than by direction make it harder for youth to see relevance in college studies."

Believing that " 'Bachelor of Arts' at present means little or nothing as a symbol of liberal education," the president of Claremont Graduate School and University Center, in this speech before the National Conference of Academic Deans, meeting in Los Angeles on January 16, 1967, proposed a moratorium on the A.B. degree. The granting of degrees would not be abandoned: "Colleges could confer instead a baccalaureate in each major field or in a division. Thus we would have at commencement time so many Bachelors of Chemistry, Bachelors of English, of Political Science, Psychology, and so on." With such specialized baccalaureates in the major fields, an "A.B. program might then be directed toward a certain deliberate wealth and breadth of study."

If the motives of students and professors are wide apart, as Dr. Benezet believes, then "it is time to cease merely accelerating student efforts, and to start directing that effort toward the broad intellectual growth we all say may yet become the salvation of human society."

Students interested in further examination of college unrest and activism are invited to read Nathan Glazer's stimulating article entitled "Student Politics in a Democratic Society," which appeared in the Spring 1967 issue of the *American Scholar,* pages 202-17.

The war between students and teachers has reached a curious turn. It is a very old war, perhaps next oldest to the war between men and women as chronicled by James Thurber. One of the earliest cuneiform fragments we have from the fertile crescent of the Near East consists of a discussion of unruly pupils and what the teacher should do to control them.

The curious turn in the student-versus-teacher war is that neither side seems aware it is going on. True enough, certain battle slogans are being hurled back and forth between the two camps. Over the past decade the teachers' war cry has been, "Excellence." This cowed the students for a while; but in the past two years they have summoned their forces enough to hurl back their own rebel yell, likewise consisting of one word, "Relevance!"

Despite such three-syllable encounters neither the students nor the teachers are yet willing to admit they are at war with one another. Professors by and large claim that students were never more willing to work hard. A prevailing faculty legend is that students are coming from high school so well prepared in their subjects that the first two years of college bore them stiff. Like most generalities about college education, the claim is innocent of statistics. It is formed mainly by impressions of individual students from superior high schools, and typifies the noonday conversational fare at the Faculty Club.

Students on their part are not saying the faculty are at war with them. How can one be at war with a force he seldom sees? In general, students are not even militant about inaccessible or nonteaching professors. They are more inclined to believe that the war is with their particular college or university itself, as captioned by that gloomy abstraction of all compounded error, *the administration.*

The student cry for relevance is most often phrased in terms of their own freedoms. Restrictions upon their conduct or their political activity are held out as proof that the university lives in a bygone age. Only recently and in isolated cases have students directed their claims for relevance at the teaching program itself.

Thus we ride on an academic carrousel. Presidents and deans chase after professors pleading with them to teach more but rewarding them for teaching less. Professors chase students with tighter academic requirements and more specialized subject matter, under the banner of excellence. Students chase the administration asking for more freedoms on and off the campus. They are only dimly aware that their freedom-desires may be more in reaction to academic pressures than to institutional constraints. (The Muscatine report of the select faculty committee at Berkeley made this explicit, but the public has largely missed the point.) Seldom does any one think, much less try, to spin the carrousel back the other way.

The motion of our academic carrousel is accelerating. Part of the acceleration is due to the driven energies of the people on board. As students clamor for freedoms from the administration, presidents and deans plead harder for professors to draw nigher to students and calm them down. As professors translate such appeals into their language of additional academic requirements, the students accept the additional charge but then press for unbridled indulgences in their remaining hours free from study. There are dynamics enough in the carrousel to make it spin faster as a result of its own workings.

Yet there is also an outside motor driving the carrousel, and it too is accelerating. Contemporary society is accelerating. The condition was diagnosed sixty years ago by Henry Adams, who expressed his relief that he was due to get off at that time. Compared with the pace of life in 1900, how would he describe life in 1967?

It is not the sheer speed of existence that is so wearing. Our increased dependence upon bigness and mechanical controls to manage our existence threatens to chew up human beings in the process. Recently the United States lost through violence a President who, whether accurately or inaccurately, symbolized humanistic ideals for much of the country's youth. Before his death America had become involved in an undeclared war ten thousand miles away. The justness of that war continues to confuse us. But there is no confusion in the instant, pitiless communication of horror brought to the civilians of that war—nothing new to war true enough, but never before so starkly presented to our own civilians in living TV color. Meanwhile, the impacted peoples of our inner cities press for a reinterpretation of humanity for them too. Let us face it: the 1960's have not been a vintage decade for humanism, except in what has been shown to be lacking. This is affecting education more than we realize.

The attritions of a society characterized by velocity rather than by direction make it harder for youth to see relevance in college studies. Kenneth Keniston, who wrote about twelve bright disaffected Harvard students, reports over and over in his book, *The Uncommitted,* the students' belief that the quality of human life is going downhill; and that their claim against Harvard was that the University seemed to them as part of a vast establishment which is permitting the downgrading of human values to happen.

Just how serious is the student unrest today?

As usual in questions concerning college education, reliable generalizations are yet few. Twelve disaffected Harvard youths do not an epidemic make; nor do even three thousand student protesters in Berkeley. Still, the most casual observation will reveal that there is more student demonstrating in more American colleges than has gone on in recent decades. Some educators believe it is a good thing, indicating that students have left the last of the so-called silent generation following the GI boom after World War II.

More serious is the strong evidence that students individually are more disturbed, more wracked by anxiety, more inclined to leave college in search of meaning, and less receptive to organized campus life in its various forms. There is a workaday grimness about today's students; it is too often reported not to be a datum. Certain colleges advertise that 75 to 80 per cent of their A.B.'s go on to graduate school. Among these however, the businesslike grimness may be even more pronounced. Progress through a selective liberal arts college can indeed become a business; and the high percentage

going on to graduate school conceivably reflects more the acceptance of a class conformity than spontaneous intellectual drive.

Anybody can recite symptoms and argue about their meaning.
Enough here to assert that student tension is up on the American
campus; that it is a serious condition; and that administrators ought
to study it more systematically than they are now doing.

If, beyond this, a plus correlation can be seen between student
demands for relevance and the narrowing of undergraduate teaching by specialism, then the rest of my argument may be of some use.

For the student already happily intent upon his specialty, increasing academic rigor may serve as a compliment, a sort of early
invitation into the scholar's guild. But for the student, typically the
sophomore, unsure of what he wants or how much of a specialty,
or just why he is in college at all, increasing the academic rigor
amounts to going past the rack on which the student feels already
stretched and giving it a friendly turn. To change the figure, it can
become like dousing a fire with kerosene.

Something like this I submit is happening. Couple it with the
increasing depersonalization on campuses both small and large, as
academic methods become more mechanized and as professors dig
into their own pursuits, assisted by liberal leave policies. Couple it
again with a world scene in which deprived peoples both at home
and abroad are crying injustice against the power of the American
technology, and we have both negative and positive poles for a
new student identification. When that identification has not yet
lodged itself with the academic setting or process, the alternative
may be eagerly grasped. The student sums things up on campus
with the challenge word, relevance. He may not actually leave college; he may spiritually leave it, even if his physical moves are con-
fined to strumming protest songs through the night at his favorite
off-campus pad.

The residential undergraduate liberal arts college, to be sure,
has higher scores than any other kind for student satisfaction with
faculty teaching, as studies by Robert Pace and others show. In almost all colleges moreover much effort is going toward enriching
the campus milieu with lectures, films, forums, and exhibits on

world issues. Yet as Lewis Mayhew has pointed out, it somehow remains peripheral to what students consider the pay-off of college experience. The sad fact persists that in all our decades of college reforms—and there have been some—we have scarcely budged an inch from the overriding faculty criterion of success for student response: *grades.* Concerning grades Robert Pace, a researcher in student response, supplied the following clincher in his paper for the 1965 American Council on Education Annual Meeting:

> Academic grades predict academic grades and scholastic aptitude tests predict scholastic performance. But neither has much relationship to anything else—not creativity, not inventiveness, not leadership, not good citizenship, not compassion, not esthetic sensitivity, not expressive talent in any of the performing arts, not personal and social maturity, not mental health, not vocational success, not family happiness, not honest workmanship. Yet are we not concerned with these things too . . .?

As W. H. Auden wrote in another context, "We have heard these words before, and we shall hear them again. . . ." My discussion will try to avoid the rest of the litany, whose form requires invocations before a familiar pantheon of educational gods. We might try instead to review the human elements of any college setting and look for realistic ways for effecting change.

The easiest place to start change in college, since it is the faculty who are expected to initiate action, is to change the student. This we attempt by refining the admission-screening and tightening the academic requirements for degrees. Theoretically we should arrive at length at a student body whose intellects and desires are identical with those of their professors. In a very few colleges—perhaps a dozen in the country—this for practical purposes is being accomplished. (It might be footnoted, in those colleges we are also experiencing some of the strongest student tensions, presumably from the friction of all-out competition.)

The trouble is, nature in each generation produces only a certain proportion of people whose minds and temperaments crave the unalloyed academic life. If a college screens out all others, it merely leaves the vast majority to be educated elsewhere by colleges either less capable of being quite so selective or inclined by other motives not to be so. Thus the big job of college motivation remains to be done for young people who will serve out their years in careers other than as professional scholars. This includes an increasing number who through social pressures of various kinds are going on to graduate school. Graduate education is increasingly required for many careers. Yet it is not accurate to equate the rise in graduate students with an increase of intellectuality *per se*. Some highly practical vocational reasons are involved, more and more each year. (The influence of the military draft is another negative incentive whose strength may be variously assessed.)

In brief, we cannot change a whole student generation by cranking up requirements in this or that college. We *can* charge a student generation in all colleges to face the more genuine incentives of higher learning.

The real change we seek in a student is to hasten that moment when he sees beyond his self-image into a world for the first time made visible in the light of some striking idea. What we would wish is for that student from such experience to resolve to be a lifelong learner in whatever he takes on, be it academic, occupational, social or esthetic. Such changes are not wrought by placing demands upon the student alone.

To speak of "changing the professor" as analogous to changing the student might be termed *infra dig*, especially in the light of a current sellers' market for faculty. Logan Wilson's book, *The Academic Mind*, now twenty-five years old, reminds us that professors by and large are people and that decade in and decade out they respond to the incentives of their times. At present, administrators in the ranking institutions seem unable or unwilling, or both, to arrange incentives for faculty in a direction opposite to their self-advancement as professional scholars. The knowledge industry has dictated that; and it bids fair to increase. If one is to believe such a one as Marshall McLuhan (that is, if he presumes to understand McLuhan at all), knowledge will become in the future the basic unit of economic production.

There are, however, professors in all our colleges who when even reasonably encouraged will give their energies to teaching and counseling students both brilliant and ordinary. They will respond to invitations for broadening a subject so as to present what Daniel Bell calls its conceptual innovations, rather than a mere inventory of its data.

The administrator's question remains, how can such invitations best be made?

Professor Bell's prize-winning book, *The Reforming of General Education,* goes exhaustively into discussions for reorganizing the college curriculum in order that the student may experience real intellectual growth, instead of a swelling of facts and theories briefly retained. With his own Columbia as reference, Bell presents courses and sequences in a logical order so as to make for the growth of concepts, in the spirit of Jerome Bruner's cognitive theories of learning.

Professor Bell's discussion has great value, especially in the sociological setting for college today which he supplies. Its main difficulties are two. For all its clarity it is a professor's essay written for professors (his fifth chapter on curriculum building is particularly so). As such it shows not much promise of ever breaking out of the faculty forensic circle or of reforming the specialists who teach. Its proposals thus could die aborning, just as the so-called Redbook general education plan of Harvard, which Bell quotes extensively, died of anemia after some ten years of faculty phlebotomy and the failure of academic administrators to come to its aid.

The second difficulty is that in learning, that which is logical may not be psychological; and what may be psychological for the learning of students at Columbia, Harvard and Chicago may not be psychological for students of, say, Iowa State, Whitman and Rice. In his introduction, Bell acknowledges the omission of data concerning "the changing concerns of the student body and the character of their demands." His bibliography lists no references of contemporary research into students' social psychology: studies by Newcomb of Michigan, Sanford of Vassar and Stanford, or of Stern, Pace, Heist, Trow, Webster and others. To write a curriculum study today without reference to such findings is like writing a pharmacopoeia without reference to anatomy or physiology. It continues the history of doctors of higher learning, of whom Robert Hutchins was for long chief of staff, who over the decades have been too busy formulating their prescriptions to take time to examine a patient. (Despite these difficulties, Bell has written a brilliant essay about general education, which is a step ahead of his time among selective college faculties.)

In the final summing-up, the most that a college can wish for is that as a result of its four-year program it can demonstrate growth in intellectual interests and skills among the majority of its students. The chance to do this lies in keeping a consistency between its aims for a liberal education and the methods it uses. Toward that end I conclude with a proposal for the entire college profession.

What I propose is a national moratorium on the A.B. degree. I would have this pending a study of its true meaning and definition for modern times. It is time to admit that "Bachelor of Arts" at present means little or nothing as a symbol of liberal education.

Degree-granting itself need not be suspended. (Small danger that it would be. Dean Gordon Whaley of the University of Texas has counted 2,500 different degrees in use in the United States.) Colleges could confer instead a baccalaureate in each major field, or in a division. Thus we would have at commencement time so many Bachelors of Chemistry, Bachelors of English, of Political Science, Psychology, and so on. For those with broader programs we could confer the Bachelor of Humanities, of Science, or of Social Science.

Repugnant though such proliferated degrees may sound, they would only reflect, in effect, the kind of degrees most colleges are giving now.

These specific degrees could then serve as entree to graduate school, where in due course the Masters in Economics, Zoology, etc. might be surmounted by a new terminal professional degree, Doctor of Economics, or Zoology. The M.A. and the Ph.D. programs on the other hand I would reserve for the same national study proposed for the Bachelor of Arts.

College discussions today involve whether the Ph.D., which is a research degree, can ever be redefined to reflect broad preparation;

or whether for college teaching a substitute degree without dissertation requirement might be accepted by the college world. History lends little hope for the latter, and I am not sure it should. The former idea—broadening the Ph.D. itself—might be possible if we were to substitute another doctorate which gives full rein to specialized research. This exists now in some applied fields but they are not well recognized (at least one institution has conferred, for example, the degree, Doctor of Rural Engineering). If some university were to begin conferring the Doctor of Chemistry degree, Doctor of Political Science, Doctor of Romance Languages and so on, the way would be cleared for a Doctorate of Philosophy of genuine breadth. I am sure once again such a change would not be popular; it would at least be honest.

Let us consider again the Bachelor of Arts. With new, specialized baccalaureates in the respective major fields clearing out the student who wants to hasten on to his profession, the A.B. might then be directed toward a certain deliberate wealth and breadth of study.

First, we might ban acceleration (except for the mature returning adult) on the basis that liberal education is not susceptible to forced draft. We might then insist on four residential years, with summers away from formal study.

Second, we might discourage majors for some students, and in any event, not require majors.

Third, the mechanical distribution requirement for courses in all three divisions could be changed or ended. It is already being dropped in some colleges. This is not to abandon the objective of general education. General education is possible within even one academic field provided the student can be led far enough to see the implications of that field for other fields, which he then may elect on his own to study. It may be time to declare the formal general education system dead in America: to cease bowing to its corpse, and to pursue the spirit of broad learning in fresher ways. Mechanical general education requirements have never really worked; why not admit it?

Requirements to take introductory courses in all three major divisions were first introduced sixty years ago. Students still speak of them as something to get over, like a childhood disease. A year later, the retention factor for many is nil. In some of the new English universities efforts are being made to teach general education by broad courses within the student's subject division. They rely upon the intellectual life of the campus to carry him beyond that. The big need in our colleges is not so much for a broader curriculum, but for broader teachers.

Fourth, we might ask each candidate for a Bachelor of Arts to submit in his last year an original paper or project which draws from at least two different subject areas.

Fifth, we might plan more systematically than we do now to integrate students into the life and governance of the college. We could fight depersonalization by building instruction around the residential unit. Claremont has experimented with this for forty years. It is heartening to see large universities now trying the same thing.

What could preserve such an A.B. program from formlessness or even quackery?

Clearly a faculty adviser system worthy of the name would be involved. Clearly also some plan of broad examination would be necessary.

Considering the growing size of college units, the examinations would have to be standardized. Here lies a rub, if we want to teach for concept rather than coverage. Yet we have barely begun on the potentialities for the examination of concept. Moreover, most college teacher-to-student ratios are high enough to make oral examinations feasible in addition, perhaps in groups of two or three students. Remember that many students would have elected degree programs in specific fields rather than a Bachelor of Arts which carries out its meaning. Such an A.B. in fact would probably become an honors degree. Nothing would be more appropriate for a Bachelor of Arts. It could then become the cornerstone for a new Master of Arts, and for a new Doctor of Philosophy.

I realize I have described something like the A.B. program at the University of Chicago twenty-five years ago, minus the required general courses of that day (another difference is that Chicago had no alternative specialized degrees such as I have suggested). After twenty-five hundred years of higher education it is not easy to propose something new. But good old ideas become forgotten.

Whatever the merits of an A.B. program protected from the inroads of specialism, a moratorium on present practices is needed. We should have a thorough national study of the A.B. comparable to the historic Flexner report on medical education in the early twentieth century.

Meanwhile, students in college are restless. In my judgment there has not been a period in recent decades when the personal motives of students and the personal motives of professors were wider apart. If that is even partly true, it is time to start closing the gap. It is time to cease merely accelerating student effort, and to start directing that effort toward the broad intellectual growth we all say may yet become the salvation of human society .

WHY NATIONAL CONCERN FOR BIOMEDICAL COMMUNICATION? [3]

Seymour M. Farber, M.D. [4]

Much has been written about what C. P. Snow called the "gulf of mutual incomprehension" between the literary intellectuals and the physical scientists. With increasing specialization, the difficulties in communication extend beyond the polar extremes of scientists and nonscientists. Within each group, professionals find it hard to convey their meanings to others outside their narrow specialties. The audience for certain high-level inquiries becomes precious small, and the attempts to make the layman understand what is said are not uniformly successful.

The sophisticated data of the specialties and subspecialties—and the attendant challenges of sharing their meanings with ordinary people—have resulted in a kind of selective communication in which only the experts in the fragmented fields know what the other experts are saying.

The communication of specialized information has many facets. And it is always heartening to hear from the authority who views communication as a broad spectrum extending far beyond the hard data of a scientific area understandable only to a relatively few, and embracing additionally the insights afforded by the humane disciplines. The speech reprinted below is a case in point. Delivered in New York City by Dr. Seymour M. Farber on April 4, 1966, at a conference on biomedical communication sponsored by the New York Academy of Sciences and the Public Health Service Audiovisual Facility, this address presents a clear and precise message:

> We in biomedical communication must not forget that the information required by the practicing clinician originates not only in a biochemistry laboratory, but also from a sociological investigation and from the insights of cultured minds.
>
> Without a multidisciplinary approach to multidimensional man we cannot minister to the total and real health needs of man. To employ the health findings of science without humane reservations is to devalue the individuality of man which made us interested in helping him in the first place.

[3] Conference on Biomedical Communication: Problems and Resources, sponsored by the New York Academy of Sciences and the Public Health Service Audiovisual Facility, New York City, April 4, 1966. Text furnished by Dr. Farber, with permission for this reprint.

[4] For biographical note, see Appendix.

Dr. Farber concluded that "health information should be effectively communicated to the widest possible audience and on a regular basis." Moreover,

> . . . if we promulgate a view of health which is restricted only to "hard data," will we elicit concern among the public at large? I suggest that a biomedical communication which deals with man in his totality can elicit support because this is a message that is understandable to people who are perhaps becoming suspicious of a strictly technical, dehumanized approach to health.

Dean of Educational Services and Director of Continuing Education, Medicine and Health Services at the San Francisco Medical Center of the University of California, Dr. Farber endorses a realistic view of biomedical communication because "it attempts to deal with people as they actually live their lives and it does so in a way that they can understand."

Interested students are invited to examine another of Dr. Farber's addresses, "Greatest Challenge in Medicine Today," reprinted in the *Journal of the American Medical Association*, August 9, 1965, pages 432-5.

To deny the importance of biomedical communication at a gathering such as this would be tantamount to contesting the primacy of virtue over vice. As a matter of fact, I agree that biomedical communication is essential to the health sciences, that it ought to be improved, and I also agree that there is legitimate reason to be concerned over presently inadequate methods of disseminating medical information. But I believe that our concern should include the type of information we are seeking to communicate, as well as the methods we use for communication.

The point that will be made here is that "hard" technical data is a necessary, but insufficient prerequisite to achieving and maintaining the highest possible standard of medical practice. In other words, the "hard data" of clinical medicine and the basic health sciences constitutes only one part of the problem of biomedical communication. There is also a need for national concern about biomedical communication in a broader and indispensable sense which is seriously lacking today. However, before this other aspect of health information is examined, I would like to discuss some features of the communication problem as it is ordinarily considered.

The increase of technical information in clinical medicine and the biological sciences, particularly in the past twenty years, has been extraordinary. A partial measure of the burgeoning amount of data can be seen in the fact that in 1964, the National Library of Medicine received more than 18,500 different journals, only a very small portion of which have been indexed. And the *Index Medicus* for 1964 contained more than 145,000 entries, an increase of almost 9 per cent over the previous year. Even if this rate of progress in the health sciences should remain constant, which it will not, it has been estimated that a major portion of any undergraduate medical curriculum becomes significantly obsolete every five years.

This obsolescence is due not only to the sheer amount of information being reported, although there is enough to test the pertinacity of an army of insatiably curious physicians. A more important factor is the nature of the technical information which must be assimilated. The increasing importance of molecular biology illustrates this point.

Using extremely precise investigative tools and techniques, our attention has turned from a particular diseased organ to the molecular basis of the disease process itself. Physicians must therefore command a knowledge not only of specific organs, but of the dynamic biochemical and physiological relationships existing between entire systems of organs. As a consequence, today's doctor must learn how to make his way through increasingly difficult technical data in order to apply the results of the "new medicine" in clinical practice. And with each new advance in research, efficient communication between investigator and clinician becomes more important because it is by means of this communication that a transition between new discovery and implementation is made. It cannot be said often enough that the degree to which this communication is faulty, is also the degree to which potential cures are not realized.

Unfortunately, there are other factors which are impeding the translation of "hard" health data into practical medicine. At the very time that medicine is becoming more difficult, the population is growing larger and the supply of trained health personnel is, relatively speaking, growing smaller. In our state of California, for example, we expect that by 1975 the population will have increased by over 30 per cent to just under 24 million. The national projection also indicates a considerable, if not so spectacular, population increase. But the national ratio of physicians per 100,000 population has remained nearly constant for the past thirty years. And this leaves out of account the growing shortage of other health personnel —dentists, pharmacists, nurses, and medical technicians.

This dual pressure of increasing knowledge and growing population is making it difficult for the physician to resist not only professional obsolescence, but also impersonalization in his treatment of patients. What is to be the physician's recourse when his clinical load increases even over what it is today? And of course the clinical load will increase under Medicare and under the Medical Complexes program. Further, in a changing social structure we can anticipate a substantial change in the level of acceptable treatment. An increasingly urbanized population will not be long in appreciating the significance of a statement by a member of the Presidential Commission on Heart Disease, Cancer, and Stroke, "Just by applying what we know, we could save half of the people who contract cancer."

There is another situation which is inhibiting communication of "hard data" and consequently, clinical application of this data. It has been a natural response to increasing biomedical complexity that extreme specialization has arisen. There is not a field of medicine without its specialties and subspecialties—each of which is reporting advances in diagnosis and therapy. Inevitably, a technical jargon develops and new findings are described in terms which are readily comprehensible to fewer and fewer physicians. This is serious enough, but technical specialization can also make a physician hesitant to treat even a simple condition which is outside of his own medical specialty.

Now factors such as those mentioned tend to widen the gap between discovery of scientific facts and their clinical implementation. But the brute mechanical problem of narrowing the gap between discovery and application is not new. There is, for example, the almost unbelievable case of the Chinese work *Neiching* or *Canon of Medicine,* which contains the following statement, "All the blood of the body is under control of the heart and flows in a continuous circle and never stops." The *Neiching* was written in 2697 B.C., 4300 years before Harvey's "discovery."

A more modern instance is that of sulfanilamide, which was identified from a compound first synthesized in 1908 by Gelmo and described in his doctoral thesis as "para-amino-benzene-sulfonamide." It took thirty years and the work of Domagk at I. G. Farben, Colbrook in London, and finally Trefouëls at the Pasteur Institute, before we really had our first "wonder drug." But for thirty years, Gelmo's discovery lay unnoticed and unused.

The classical example of this phenomenon concerns the bacteriologist Fleming, who in 1928 accidentally noticed that a mold which had mysteriously formed in one of his petrie dishes was inhibiting the growth of bacteria. He duly published his finding in 1929, but nothing was done about it medically, until 1939 by Florey and Chain; and by 1942—fourteen years after his first observation—Fleming cured a personal friend dying of meningitis with penicillin.

The time intervening between these discoveries and their application is footnoted with curable patients whose death was the penalty for inadequate medical communication.

Clearly, the problem of translating scientific discovery into clinical medicine is not new. What is new is the marvelous techniques we have devised to aid in the translating. But more important, there is the growing belief that translation of hard scientific data into clinical medicine is the principal, if not sole, means of achieving good health. My disagreement with this point of view could not be more fundamental.

To be sure, the plethora of hard data and the intrinsic nature of this data, lends itself to quantification and hence to mechanically efficient means of communication. Pre-eminent among mechanical devices is of course the computer. But suppose we invested a few hundred million dollars to devise reliable and tested magnetic tapes describing all that is right and all that is wrong with each physiological system of the human body. Grant that this were achieved and that we then allocated even more sums for the construction of computational diagnostic centers throughout the country and instructed local physicians in accepted procedures for drawing upon the data retrieval systems built into these centers. Would the diagnostic and therapeutic information thus retrieved and preponderantly relied upon make for a state of health which patients—and physicians—would find acceptable? Would this information by itself really make for good "bedside" medicine?

These questions do not imply a kind of medical Ludditism directed against the villainous computer. Neither are they intended to detract from the value of other techniques for conveying the latest scientific data to practitioners. Far from it. I have devoted over a decade of work to continuing education in medicine, in which we have used as many means as possible for getting the latest data and techniques to practitioners. These include over one hundred courses in clinical medicine, three medical radio broadcasts a week, and we are now actively planning a medical television series. But is this the full extent of the communication problem in medicine? Is this fundamentally all that is required for good health and should it be the limit of our concern in biomedical communication?

When a patient visits a physician, he does so as a multidimensional human being who lives in a total environment and is affected by many elements in that environment. He is not simply a collection of symptoms, which are to be sorted and sifted by solid-state circuitry, and an evaluation then announced via flashing colored lights on a master control console. This restriction of "health information" to "hard" scientific data, whether the means of conveyance is the computer, radio, television, or the journals, in fact, results in a limited contribution to good health.

This is so because the paramount issue in medicine is still concerned with a meeting between two people—the patient and the physician. And in this meeting the good doctor shows the deepest understanding he is capable of; he tries to see the whole patient by using all the information he can gather; he tries to make his patient feel better—in the best sense of those words. When he does this he is attempting to achieve and maintain a standard of health in keeping with the definition of the World Health Organization:

Health is a state of complete physical, mental, and social well-being and not merely the absence of disease or infirmity. Health in this complete sense cannot be achieved if biomedical data is made rigidly synonymous with "hard" scientific data. And if biomedical communication is to make its most complete contribution to good health, its concern cannot be restricted to the impersonal data of science.

This point was especially well put by Dr. John Saunders, Chancellor of the University of California Medical Center in San Francisco. Dr. Saunders wrote that advances in medical science will be implemented in a

social structure which is objectively complex and growing more so each day. . . . This complexity and subtlety affects every doctor-patient relationship whether we acknowledge it or not. It is better that we do. To make the most complete diagnosis of a patient and then to render the best treatment, the physician must take into account not only the laws of physiology, but also all the social factors which influence and affect the health of his patient. To do this job well, the doctor of tomorrow will have to be part scientist, part clinician, part humanist, and in the fullest possible measure.

This, in my opinion, is an estimable ideal for medicine, and by extension, a necessary guideline for any system of biomedical communication. I also believe that the attainability of the ideal outweighs our reluctance to accept it.

Those of us who are interested in improving biomedical communication must therefore continue to seek the widest possible dissemination of technical information in order to forestall obsolescent treatment. But, and this is my main point, we must also learn how to relate this information to the complete and entire man in order to achieve the best medicine. Operationally, this means that the data communicated to health professionals must come from two sources: science and the humanities.

Extending the base of relevant medical information is an approach as old as Hippocrates. The horizons of ancient medicine were extended when Hippocrates observed that the achievement and maintenance of health requires more than bloodletting, drugs, and the knife. Man's health, he told us, also depends on other factors —the food he eats, the air he breathes and the water he drinks, whether he lives near a swamp or in an arid climate, at low elevations or high. We too must extend our medical horizons.

When we investigate the clinical effects of vitamin A on a rat colony, the rat's feelings do not concern us; but when we treat man, his feelings do and must concern us. Can we meaningfully and significantly speak of "cures," without taking into account the influence of man's loneliness and his gregariousness; his stress and his adaptability; his neurosis and his resiliency; his attitudes about society and the nature of that society; in short, the total culture with which he interacts and which acts upon him? Have we achieved the best medicine if we "cure" our patient only to find that he wishes we hadn't?

To gain an insight and better understanding of these dimensions of man's life requires that our "health data" recognize the validity and importance of the learned disciplines which study these dimensions: the arts, literature, philosophy, and the social sciences.

But humanistic studies are important not only for the intrinsic pleasures they can give us. They are also one of the most practical regimens yet devised for elucidating, developing, and understanding the inner man and his relationship to the world in which he lives. In our time, this humanistic information is as necessary an adjunct to our laboratory data as an understanding of Hippocrates' work *Airs, Waters, Places* was to sixth-century Greek surgery.

When a housecall is made in the middle of the night, we know, we hope, that all the medicine is not in the little black bag. Can anyone really doubt that the most scientifically trained man who carries that little black bag will be a more effective physician if he really understands why he has made that call, what he is trying to achieve, and most important, if he has a grasp of the totality of the object of that call—the patient? And is not this kind of self-knowledge and insight furthered by communicating with the minds of men who can meaningfully contribute to the doctor's understanding and experience? We in biomedical communication must not forget that the information required by the practicing clinician originates not only in a biochemistry laboratory, but also from a sociological investigation and from the insights of cultured minds.

Without a multidisciplinary approach to multidimensional man we cannot minister to the total and real health needs of man. To employ the health findings of science without humane reservations is to devalue the individuality of man which made us interested in helping him in the first place.

Massive expenditures for institutionalized research have resulted in an enormous amount of scientific data with which we have attained extraordinary success against somatic morbidity. But in this process, we seem to have forgotten that the goal of medicine, and hence, of medical communication is not only to cure, but to alleviate human suffering whenever possible and to comfort always.

Biomedical communication in this broader sense is not receiving national concern—at least not as much as it should. However, I do not wish to present a distorted picture. Meetings and discussions such as this one are certainly a step in the right direction. But, we must be unceasing in our efforts to make broader humanistic issues an established part of the biomedical dialogue. In short, it is incumbent on biomedical communication to provide the means by specialists in all fields of learning and areas of achievement.

It is unlikely that there is a single best technique for doing this. But the kind of thing that is possible can be illustrated by specific example. At the Medical Center in San Francisco, we have been holding two-day-long symposia several times a year, which are open to layman and physician alike. Our "faculty" for these symposia has included sociologists and lawyers, surgeons and psychiatrists, economists and pediatricians, historians and anthropologists, political theorists and philosophers, newspaper columnists, authors, politicians, demographers, pharmacologists, and biochemists. These outstanding men and women have come from all parts of the United States and from throughout the world to speak, and I believe their audiences have profited by listening to them.

The titles of a few symposia will indicate the variety of subjects that can be covered: Man Under Stress; The Air We Breathe; Food and Civilization; Control of the Mind; The Family's Search for Survival; Alcohol and Civilization; Teen-Age Marriage and Divorce; The Dilemmas of Sex Education; The Challenge to Women—The

Biologic Avalanche, etc. These programs have been broadcast and televised, live and taped, on both domestic networks and on the Voice of America throughout the world. And to make the discussions available to the largest possible audience, many of the proceedings have been published in book form.

This aspect of health is as legitimate a part of medical communication as a notice of the latest data on antibiotics. I am not speaking of a hierarchy of importance. But if we wish to treat the patient as he really is, we cannot afford to overlook the nontechnical factors in his environment which affect his reality. Further, I suggest that this approach to biomedical communication can contribute to a sense of professional integrity and fulfillment which an exclusive reliance on "hard data" cannot do, no matter how rigorously or systematically presented.

It cannot be denied that this view of biomedical communication involves problems. There is for example the question of how to support a broader program. However, my experience in biomedical communication—and as a practicing physician—has taught me at least this much: reluctant support is one of the hazards of the game, just as insufficient time is a problem in clinical practice. In each case the solution is essentially the same—we have to make even greater efforts to find it. However, we must remember that the more imagination and energy we expend in making complete biomedical communication an established and recognized part of medical education, the easier it will be to acquire support. It is principally through our own efforts that this goal will be achieved.

But finances are not the paramount consideration because better health does not necessarily follow from gross expenditures of money—it also requires people. Biomedical communication must be made attractive to the highest caliber professionals in all capacities and in all disciplines. We must work toward the day when a career in biomedical communication has a professional status as reputable as that in electron microscopy. When our programs and purposes are good enough, they will attract more of the best people —and these will attract support.

Underlying these practical considerations is the basic approach we must take. We all agree that health information should be effectively communicated to the widest possible audience and on a regular basis. But if we promulgate a view of health which is restricted only to "hard data," will we elicit concern among the public at large? I suggest that a biomedical communication which deals with man in his totality can elicit support because this is a message that is understandable to people who are perhaps becoming suspicious of a strictly technical, dehumanized approach to health.

In a world in which we can no longer afford the luxury of disregarding man's relationship to his fellows and to his environment, there must indeed be an involved commitment to biomedical communication. But the health information communicated must include any and all data from sciences and the humanities that can contribute to good health. I believe that this is a realistic view of biomedical communication because it attempts to deal with people as they actually live their lives and it does so in a way that they can understand. A concern for biomedical communication in this sense was needed yesterday, it is desperately wanted today. Without this concern for the whole man, our attempts to cope with the genuine human problems of tomorrow may prove to be unavailing and irrelevant. The time has come for medicine and medical communication to make their greatest possible contributions to the total man in his environment.

IS GOD OVER THIRTY?
RELIGION AND THE YOUTH REVOLT [5]

David H. C. Read [6]

Youth must be very much flattered to see so many people discuss so
many facets of what the elders, both out of fear and astonishment, call the
problem of the new generation. This circumstance recently prompted one
of my friends to remark, with a kind of rueful self-pity, that he awaited
the happy day when someone would again write or speak about the plight
of the middle-aged. Passing the age of thirty, he felt, was like picking up
one's passport to oblivion. And evidently he doubted that the passport was
renewable.

Doubtless the young student groups have received the major share of
publicity during the mid-sixties, largely because they were vocal, articulate,
concentrated in centers of intellectual ferment, and motivated in the main
by laudable hopes and ideals. The most vigorous activists have indeed
distressed a segment of our population—in fact may even have frightened
it. Understandably, people who are anything but timid may have trouble
occasionally in spotting the difference between activism addressed to the
attainment of defensible goals and irresponsible noise-making that seems
to derive from no discernible issue. Keen observers of the college scene—
notably Clark Kerr, former president of the University of California at
Berkeley—surmise that changes in the ways of the activists are taking
place, however, and that with the upcoming generation "confrontation
politics . . . may face an early decline."

Be that as it may, the students' search for identity—in fact, youth's
search, in or out of school—goes on. And this is the urgent call for understanding among all groups, regardless of age. Significantly, youth enjoys,
with exceptions of course, the sympathetic understanding and support of its
elders. By and large, government, industry, and the professions at their
most responsible levels are on the side of youth, and are ready to jump to
its defense whenever it is maligned or attacked. And the speech reprinted
below is not unrepresentative of such defense.

The Rev. Dr. David H. C. Read has since 1956 been minister at the
Madison Avenue Presbyterian Church in New York City. Scottish-born,

[5] Madison Avenue Presbyterian Church, New York City, April 9, 1967. Text furnished
by Dr. Read, with permission for this reprint.
[6] For biographical note, see Appendix.

Dr. Read is a strong speaker with a good sense of timing. He engages difficult and sensitive topics with directness and economy of style. In this speech, delivered from his pulpit on April 9, 1967, he acknowledged that "there has never been a period in history when youth and age were in perfect accord." But he doubted that modern youth was actively in revolt against religion. Rather, youth was suspicious of a "packaged religion" that assumed a rigid posture and wrapped beliefs into neat parcels; and youth suspected that many of the older persons were guilty of hypocrisy. While declaring that no age group was exempt from hypocrisy, he felt sure that "we need the voice of youth to remind us of what we are really professing to believe."

When Jesus began his work he was thirty years old.—St. Luke 3:23.

. . . and in a matter of months they heard him say: "It is finished," and he was dead.

Let this be the starting-point for our thinking about religion and youth, and perhaps also for a revision of our image of God. Jesus Christ died young. He never reached middle age. Whatever he means to you, this fact has quite startling implications. If you think of him as the supreme teacher of the good life, the wisest man yet to appear on earth, then you are admitting that this wisdom was concentrated in a very young man. If you think of him as the great leader, the example for all mankind, and the one who can guide the nations into the way of peace and fulfillment, you must remember that this is being said about one who was less than half the age of the average chief of state today. If you think of him as one whose life reveals the true nature of the God and Father of us all, then you must believe that God could express all that we need to know of him in a life that barely lasted thirty years. If you hold the full faith of our creeds and confessions and believe that God really became man in Jesus Christ, that the story of his ministry, his cross, and his resurrection is the unique reconciling work of the Father Almighty, then you must believe that all this was accomplished in and through a young man. When he said: "He that hath seen me hath seen the Father," they were not looking at a venerable figure with snowy locks but at one with the physical and mental vigor of youth. What does that do to your image of God?

I begin with this, because in the current debate between youth and age (or, as the older like to say, between youth and experience) there is a tendency to line up religion with the prejudices of the old. Now it may well be that the religion we see on the surface today—the organized network of official church activities—does appear to belong to the older generation, and often indeed to be part of what youth writes off as the "Establishment." Yet Christianity, however it may be molded into the conventions of middle age from time to time, began with a young Saviour, young disciples, and a fresh and revolutionary message. And I believe that the Gospel never loses in any age its rejuvenating and recreative power. When we speak of the "revolt of youth," we should remember that this is precisely how the initial impact of Christ and his followers could be described, and how the effect of the Gospel on any of us—whatever our age—could be described today.

What, then, is this youth revolt we are talking about? Whenever I venture to assess what youth is thinking my prayer is that God will somehow prevent me from talking rubbish. And his first answer to my prayer is to remind me that there never has been a period of history when youth and age were in perfect accord.

> Said Adam to Eve,
> "I begin to perceive
> That even young Abel
> Whom we raised is unstable:
> And now it is plain
> We shall have to raise Cain."

You can find all you want about this conflict in the story of Saul and David: the jealousy of age—the old warrior didn't care for the latest song that came floating through the palace windows: "Saul has slain his thousands, but David his tens of thousands"; and later the sulky arrogance of youth as David skulked in the cave of Adullam. This generation didn't invent the generation conflict. It's built in.

I am also reminded not to spin generalizations out of the publicized activities of a segment of our youth. Since vice always is more newsworthy than virtue, and eccentricity than the daily round, the "revolt of youth" can easily conjure up a lurid picture of a whole generation on the loose—black-leathered demons on motor-bikes terrorizing a neighborhood, dope-pens where boys and girls with a maximum of hair and a minimum of clothes exchange obscenities, burn draft cards, and thumb their noses at everything their elders hold sacred. That such things happen, that there are perhaps greater excesses of lawlessness in some quarters than ever before, we know to be true. But to judge the youth of the nation on the basis of a section, mostly concentrated in the large cities, is absurd. I have no reason to believe that there is more lawlessness and immorality among the young than the middle-aged, and every reason to believe that there is, on the whole, a healthy, honest, open-minded, inquiring, good-hearted generation coming up behind us.

Wherein, then, lies the revolt? My impression is that the generation gap is somewhat greater now than in the past, and that it is not always easy for one age-group to hear what the other is saying. Therefore I want to try to listen very hard to the voice of revolt as it comes from the under-thirties—especially when it concerns the Church.

From what I read, from what I hear, and from what I sense, the youth revolt against the churches today takes two main forms. One concerns our public image as an organization, and the other our personal behavior as professed Christians.

1. The revolt of youth is against what we might call "packaged religion." There are few signs of a revolt against religion as such. On the contrary religion almost ranks with sex as a topic of conversation, and old-fashioned atheism seems definitely out. Students in state-supported colleges where formerly there was often little or no study of the subject are now flocking to courses in religion. When a friend of mine asked one Why? he got the answer: "Because that's the only place round here where ultimate issues are discussed." Concern about religion is, in fact, part of the revolt against a slick, efficient, technological society that is heading very fast towards nobody-knows-what. But a fascination with religion —whether revealed in a reading of Tillich, Buber, and Bonhoeffer,

or in a dangerous experimentation with psychedelic drugs, or the wearing of some outrageous button—is very different from enthusiasm for the Church.

The churches seem to appear as the repositories of packaged religion. With their formal services, their organization, their rules, and their rigid posture in society, they look like the very antithesis of what living religion might be. Youth, looking for the expansion of the spirit, the release of the emotions, the enlargement of consciousness that religion ought to mean, is in revolt against the neat wrappings in which we seem to present our beliefs, and the formal channels through which we seem to force the life of the spirit. With their vision of what real contact with God might be they reject the assembly-line by which they seemed to be doomed in the churches to pass from baptism through church school to confirmation and conventional membership in the pattern of their elders.

Let me dramatize this revolt for a moment. A young man stands in the middle of the avenue out there. On one side of him is a conventional church with its notices, its preachers' names, its sermon-topics, its lists of activities. On the other side a boutique with a windowful of buttons—some absurd, some witty, some satirical, some political, some religious, some just plain revolting. As he turns his back to the church the buttons become a kind of symbol of his revolt. They are not simply a gesture of defiance, deliberately calculated to shock and annoy an older generation. The religious ones are mixed in with the secular, so that even the most blasphemous indicate an obsession with the question of God. What is being rejected is the Church that we know.

If youth tells me that the Church is a religious chainstore, run by the Establishment, doling out packaged worship, packaged doctrine, packaged comfort, then I want to listen before I reply. And as I listen I hear the voice of the Hebrew prophets, of Francis of Assisi, of Martin Luther, of John Wesley, of Kierkegaard, and realize that this criticism has to be heard again and again by the Church of Christ. We *can* lose the living God in the formula of our creeds; we *can* smother the Spirit in the regularities of our liturgy; we *can* lose the reality of Christian love in the trivialities of our churchiness. The youth revolt reminds us that the Church of today is in constant danger of overorganization, of worshiping the ecclesiastical machine rather than the living God.

It is good for us to have this jolt, this apparent rejection of our accepted ways of expressing our religious faith. It is a healthy sign that serious-minded young men and women should question the forms and formulas their elders take for granted. What is not so healthy is the current reaction of the Church. For it tends to be either a sheer conservatism that defends the status quo and damns our youth as irreligious and immoral, or else a gutless liberalism that leans over backwards to join the chorus of criticism and pronounce the demise of the churches as we know them. To accept the need of reform, of renewal of a living faith, by no means implies that we are ready to jettison the faith that is the lifeblood of the Church or to tear apart the entire structure of her ministry and her worship. We have had enough of these negative critics who snipe at the Church from within, and call on us to capitulate to the spirit of the age.

What I would want to say to the youth in revolt against the established churches of our time is something like this: "You are right when you say that we sometimes give the impression of packaging the faith too neatly, and asking you to accept a form of words rather than a living Spirit. But you must remember that the Church has a specific Word about God to declare. That Word is Jesus Christ, and wherever he is proclaimed a choice comes to view. He can be accepted or rejected. We don't claim to know all about this Christ, or to interpret him infallibly. But we have been given a Gospel that centers on him, and we cannot dissolve it into some vague spirituality that is acceptable to anybody. You are right when you say that we seem to package religion in set forms and ceremonies. But have you noticed that any live movement develops its conformities? Are there not youth groups in our cities where the clothing, the language, the opinions are every bit as conformist in their own way as the average church? You can't damn the Church for its conformities unless you believe that religion is a purely private affair. What is needed is the entrance into the

Church of a youth that accepts the challenge of Christ, and is willing to move from within to reform its structures and make alive its forms and ceremonies. For the God we worship is not a patriarchal figure from the past, but the God of eternal youth."

2. The personal criticism that youth directs at the church member can be bluntly summarized: it is hypocrisy. It is a hard word, but we must face it. The young are extremely sensitive to the gap that yawns between our professions of belief and our behavior. When they say: "Never trust anyone over thirty" they are referring to the fact that, as we grow older, we tend to a kind of cynical acceptance of this gap—as if we realized that no one can really be expected to live up to all that he professes to believe. Before we resent the accusation—and who doesn't?—let's hear it humbly. They say we talk about love, but act in self-interest; that we sing about peace, but support war; that we shout about moral standards but acquiesce in glaring injustice; that we proclaim the priority of the spiritual, but order our lives by the material; that we condemn youthful promiscuity but practice the serialized polygamy of divorce. All these, and many other, charges of hypocrisy are leveled at the conventional over-thirties in our churches.

What are we to say? First, just this: that we have indeed much of which we are ashamed. If we can't say that, we are indeed hypocrites every time we repeat together a confession of sin. We must surely be humble enough to admit that there is not one of us who can claim to be living up to the highest that we know. If we do make such a claim we have never really heard the Christian Gospel. For—and this is the next thing that has to be said in all clarity—the Christian Church is the place where we come, not to be assured that we are better than our neighbors, but to place ourselves under the judgment and mercy of God. We come to hear such words as these from the thirty-year-old who surely can be trusted: "Alas for you . . . you pay tithes of mint and rue and every garden herb, but have no care for justice and the love of God . . . Alas for you . . . You love the seats of honor in churches and salutations in the marketplace . . . you are like unmarked graves over which men may walk without knowing it . . . Alas for you . . . you have taken away the key of knowledge. You did not go in yourselves, and those who were on their way in, you stopped."

The Church, in fact, can be the one place in this world where we are not able to compare ourselves favorably with someone else, because we are forced to compare ourselves with Jesus Christ. It may be true that the older we get the easier it is to dodge the challenge of the Gospel, to let the Word of God slip past us as a familiar formula, to acquiesce in a lower level of Christian life than we once aspired to. Here again we need the voice of youth to remind us of what we are really professing to believe.

But I would also ask: is there a mystic barrier at thirty that exempts the younger from any hypocrisy at all? The very charge of hypocrisy, I would remind you, is a dangerous one. It backfires. For which of us is really so omniscient as to be able to know for a fact that his brother is a hypocrite? What do we know of the secret struggles and agonies that go on in someone whom we write off as insincere? At the risk of seeming to flout this warning myself, may I not ask: Is there no hypocrisy in the claim that youth has inherited a mess it has not made? in the wholesale condemnation of a society from which so much has been received? in the slick use of slogans like: "Make love, not war"?

While it may be true that the temptations to cold conformity and to hypocrisy tend to increase with age, is it not more true that what matters is, in the end, not calendar years, but the state of the soul? There is no one here, whatever your age, who is not prone to the sins and follies we have been talking about. But there is no one here, whatever your age, who is not capable of being renewed in spirit, born again, open like a child to the grace of God in Jesus Christ. After all, it is not just to deplore our sins that we come together. It is to rejoice in the rejuvenation of the Gospel, the refreshment of the mercies that are "new every morning." In God's presence the differences of age fall away; and all can sing: "Bless the Lord, O my soul: and all that is within me, bless his holy name . . . who satisfied you with good as long as you live so that your youth is renewed like the eagle's."

Is God over thirty? We laugh at the question, and say he is ageless. But in so saying we keep the impression somehow that he must be infinitely old. To be ageless is also to be infinitely young. And it is the youthfulness of God, the modernity of his Spirit, that will in our day, as in the past, revive and renew the Church. He sees this family of his now, looking right past the surface of our years, few or many, and we know the truth of the prophetic word: "He giveth power to the faint; and to them that have no might he increaseth strength. Even the youths shall faint and be weary, and the young men shall utterly fall: but they that wait upon the Lord shall renew their strength; they shall mount up with wings as eagles; they shall run, and not be weary; and they shall walk, and not faint."

GOVERNMENT AND THE PRESS: UNEASY PARTNERS

THE FRUITFUL TENSION [1]

ROBERT F. KENNEDY [2]

Democratic Senator Robert F. Kennedy of New York is very much in the news. With the exception of President Johnson, he may possibly be getting more coverage in print than any other man in the United States. The reasons are numerous. He sustains the tradition of a proud family that has been importantly associated with public service; he carries on some of the work initiated by his brother, the late President John F. Kennedy; he appeals strongly to youth and makes a scarcely subtle bid for its support; he says controversial things; he is a fiercely partisan and dedicated politician; he is not afraid to tackle the giants; he is widely recognized as a likely candidate for President in the foreseeable future. All of which may have prompted James Reston to say that the "Kennedy story is the greatest American political phenomenon since the singing commercial, but as it changes from a lament for President Kennedy to a campaign song for Senator Robert Kennedy, it is in serious danger of being overdone."

While not an eloquent speaker, Senator Kennedy has a bit of the magical appeal that defies easy description and classification, and his major talks are sufficiently suffused with provocative, controversial material to enlist a large audience. In a speech at the University of California at Berkeley on October 22, 1966, he identified himself closely with the predominantly young audience by expressing sympathy for their "passionate concern with the condition and future of the American nation." And he spoke of the need to blend "passion, reason and courage in a personal commitment to the ideals and great enterprises of American society." Asserting that "wisdom can only emerge from the clash of contending views," he said it was not enough merely to permit dissent. "We must demand it. For there is much to dissent from."

On March 2, 1967, he demanded it. In a detailed speech on the floor of the United States Senate, Mr. Kennedy set forth a three-point plan for a settlement of the Vietnam war. The address helped to set the stage for

[1] Washington, D.C., April 23, 1967. Text furnished by Senator Kennedy, with permission for this reprint.

[2] For biographical note, see Appendix.

more extensive debate on our foreign policy in Southeast Asia. His proposal called (1) for an immediate halt to the bombing of North Vietnam; (2) for establishment of an international committee to check compliance with a request to both sides not to increase substantially "the size of the war in South Vietnam—by infiltration or reinforcement"; and (3) under United Nations direction, and with an "international presence gradually replacing American forces," for a "move toward a settlement which allows all the major political elements in South Vietnam to participate in the choice of leadership and shape their future direction as a people." Whether or not it was, as James Reston speculated, "a fuzzy and maybe even an opportunistic speech," politically and diplomatically, Senator Kennedy "more than any other presidential figure [had] at least dealt with the human agony of the war. That is something."

The speech reprinted below has a special relevancy that may enable students to understand more fully Senator Kennedy's address on Vietnam. Delivered on April 23, 1967, in Washington, D.C., before the American Society of Newspaper Editors, the address deals succinctly and perceptively with the obligations of the press and government to the people of the nation. Mindful of the delicate balance between press responsibility and national security, he believed that the press had an enviable record in its exercise of discretion in the publication of sensitive news.

For some readers, the examination of this speech will bring to mind one of the excellent addresses on a similar topic by John F. Kennedy. Almost six years previously to the day, on April 27, 1961, the late President spoke to the Bureau of Advertising of the American Newspaper Publishers Association and he too was concerned with the responsibilities of the press and government. He proposed in his talk to reconcile two seemingly contradictory requirements made necessary by the continuing national peril: "the need for far greater public information" and "the need for greater official secrecy." Soberly serious as the speech was, President Kennedy nonetheless opened his remarks with a delightful anecdote about a New York newspaper's refusal to give one of its foreign correspondents, Karl Marx, a small raise, with the consequence that the reporter ended his journalistic career and turned his talents to other causes which eventually bequeathed to the world the seeds of Leninism and the cold war.

Of all the groups that come here, yours is the most appropriate. Washington is not a center of finance or culture or industry. But it is the newspaper reading capital of the world! More people read more papers more carefully than anywhere else. We devour them for breakfast and usually end the day searching for a note of comforting flattery to help us sleep. It is the only city where a wife can anticipate her husband's mood by looking at the front page. It is a city of ten thousand proofreaders. Thus although our relationship may often waver inconstantly between anger and delight, we care about each other. Nearly every political figure harbors the hidden conviction that he could be a brilliant editor. And I suspect some editors and reporters secretly believe government would be more effective in their hands. There may be some truth to this, but of course, we must remember the last newspaper editor to become President was Warren G. Harding.

Some commentators have spoken of tension between press and government, reminiscing about gentler days. I myself deplore the violent charge of a New York governor that newspaper attacks on his administration were "scandalous, virulent and false." But that happened in 1733 and the acquittal in Governor Cosby's libel trial of editor John Peter Zenger was known as "the morning star of liberty," helping to establish the right of the press to criticize public officials. For 233 years probably not a month has gone by when some public official did not, for at least a moment, regret this decision.

However, your success is not measured by complete understanding between press and government. That is not possible, and it is probably not desirable. Nor is it found in the particular laws or policies you can influence. Yours is a more spacious and majestic part than that. In our wise and elaborate constitutional structure of checks and balances, the press is a check on government itself; giving content and meaning and force to that popular judgment and will which is the soul and design of democracy. Your obligation is not in your relationship to government but to the people; never confusing the nation with those who are its temporary leaders; serving ideas and purposes rather than men. Those of us in public life often call upon the press to be more understanding, sometimes with justice. But we also know that the day you are unanimously joined in praise of officials or policies, when power is held in awe and skepticism disappears—on that day democracy will begin to wither.

Today, as always, no movement of popular feeling and concern, whether it involves Vietnam or civil rights, poverty or pollution, is possible without the newspapers which fuel opinion, indignation and passion. You may favor policies or oppose them, condemn, protest or welcome them, yet you unavoidably sustain the limitless clash of belief from which the people derive their own judgment. In that regard you are a most powerful and necessary force of democracy.

You also guard the people's interest in less direct ways. The knowledge that hundreds are searching this city for information and that you will print what they find—whatever your political allegiance—is a potent and felt restraint. As powerfully as courts or laws, it helps ensure against the abuse and corruption of power. The wrongs and excess you expose are less important than those your very presence helps prevent. Your criticism may, at times, evoke anger, but it also deflates arrogance, which is far more dangerous.

Tonight I would like to make some brief observations about three problems which arise in the course of these responsibilities.

The first of these problems is the continuing search for a reconciliation between press responsibility and the most urgent demands of national security. I can offer you no comprehensive guide or formula; agreeing with Mr. James Reston that "there is no guiding principle to cover all cases."

The "old principle of publish-and-be-damned," Mr. Reston continues, "while very romantic . . . can often damage the national interest." The questions are enormously resistant and complex. For the issue is not simply one of secrecy. It is to decide when the government can properly ask a newspaper to suppress information because its revelation would damage the nation. The press in turn must strike a burdensome and unwelcome balance—either in response to official pleas or on its own—deciding when harm to our security outweighs the importance of public knowledge.

Clearly, publication of United States battle plans in time of war would irresponsibly imperil success and endanger American lives. On the other hand, President Kennedy once said that wider press discussion of plans to invade Cuba—known to many reporters and patriotically withheld—might have avoided the Bay of Pigs.

As you know, I have been given an opportunity to reflect on my own experience free from the pressures of executive responsibility. In looking back over crises from Berlin and the Bay of Pigs to the Gulf of Tonkin, or even over the past fifteen years, I can think of few examples where disclosure of large policy considerations damaged the country, and many instances where public discussion and debate led to more thoughtful and informed decisions.

In 1954, public response to a disclosure by the Vice President that we might intervene in Indochina, contributed to the final decision to withhold our forces. It is possible to quarrel with that judgment, but not to claim it would have been better to act in secret.

In 1961, President Kennedy met with Premier Khrushchev, hoping to reduce tensions and hostility between the two great powers. The meeting in fact was unpleasant, brutal and ominous and the failure of our expectations was not concealed. The President proclaimed no triumph of personal diplomacy and it was made clear that we should prepare for the worst. The result of candor was popular support for improved defenses and a call-up of the reserves; and a general national display of united determination which not only saw us through immediate crisis, but prepared the way for the genuine lessening of tensions that was to follow.

In 1964, when riots erupted in Panama, President Johnson freely set forth the substance of our dispute and the nature of the tensions. The subsequent public discussion dissolved the official misconception that the American people would accept no change in the status of the Panama Canal Zone, however just and reasonable. Thus we were in better position to attempt the negotiation of a new treaty, improve relations, and guard our interest in the Canal. Our dangerous difficulties with Panama had been discussed—within the government—for years. It is hard to escape the conclusion that a public debate might have created the conditions productive of action designed to avert violence.

These instances suggest a distinction which might be useful. Specific operations and methods for carrying out a publicly stated and understood policy have a high claim to secrecy, if disclosure would endanger lives or seriously impair our ability to protect our security. There is, for example, little to be gained and much to be lost by exposing a new technological device for evaluating the atomic strength of another power.

Where the question is one of policy and national direction the bias—by government and press—should be toward disclosure. If a reporter discovers the government is considering—for example— a military commitment to another country, or a change in China policy, or freer trade with Eastern Europe, then judgment would ordinarily compel publication.

There is always a tendency in government to confuse secrecy with security. Most of our historic involvement in world affairs has taken place in time of war, when secrecy was imperative. We are only slowly adjusting to the reality of continuing conflict and responsibility; and accommodating that reality to the necessities of democratic government. The power to conduct foreign affairs is freed from many of the normal checks of congressional and judicial authority. Much of this is unavoidable. However, we should not add an equal freedom from the check of public opinion. I think history demonstrates that increased revelation of the issues which engage the councils of government will frequently lead to greater public understanding and support. And even where the President feels compelled to take an unpopular decision he will act with fuller comprehension. It may be uncomfortable but it is not the purpose of democracy to ensure the comfort of its leaders.

I am aware that the distinction between method and policy will often be obscure and ambiguous. They blend imperceptibly. At times new policies must be conceived in secret, while particular operations will deserve exposure. We must ultimately depend on the sound judgment of press and government in circumstances it is impossible to foresee or describe. The record yields high confidence in the discretion of the press and its desire to serve the interests of the nation.

The second problem flows from the clash of two cherished and historic ideals—the right to a fair trial and freedom to tell the news.

It is easy, in the heat of abstract debate, to distort the real dimensions of this problem. It is not true that thousands languish innocently in prison because of newspaper assaults and irresponsibility. Such cases are undoubtedly rare. Moreover, while I was attorney general I saw many instances when press concern with crime uncovered information which helped free the innocent and exposed criminal wrong and official corruption where none suspected it.

It would be a great loss if the current debate created an array of coercive restraints designed to erect an implacable barrier between the press and the machinery of law enforcement. We must be careful in trying to protect the rights of an accused that we do not also insulate inefficiency, corruption and injustice. Those who enforce the law, like all those who exercise power in a democracy, should be subject to the guiding restraint of public knowledge, criticism and indignation.

I am confident the press itself can resolve much of the problem through voluntary application—not of artificial restraints—but the vigorous standards of good journalism. For example, it will often be inconsistent with objective reporting to publish one-sided claims by a law officer which link an accused with a crime, or an official assertion that a confession has been made. Even where a confession is undeniable, knowledge of the way it was obtained—freely or under duress, with or without knowledge of the right to keep silent and seek counsel, is essential if readers are to evaluate its legal and moral significance. It might also be both fair and wise to eliminate references to the prior criminal record, or noncriminal immorality, of an accused. At times such information may have important news values. More often it will lack such importance. At least where this is the case its publication would be inconsistent with the highest standards of fairness in journalism.

There is also much more that courts can do to avert damage from publicity. A judge can more readily defer trial at the request of a defendant until passions and publicity have faded. It should be possible to permit a more lengthy and searching examination of prospective jurors, exploring the range and intensity of their exposure to newspaper discussion. Defense attorneys could be given greater freedom to challenge jurors, if a reasonable inference of prejudice were possible. A final safeguard is the discretion of a trial judge to move a trial from any place where press coverage has been intense and prejudicial to the defendant.

Perhaps this combination of high standards of journalism and judicial discretion can help us avoid more coercive and arbitrary restrictions. In any event this should be the spirit of discussion. For the mingled values of justice and liberty are not the special interest of any group, but the common concern of the nation; and this issue is not a struggle for advantage, or a battle between bar and press, but an effort to reconcile competing aspects of democracy.

Third is the responsibility of government to give open and generous access to the press.

Once a handful of journalists could discover, comprehend and describe the major events of national politics. Today a swelling torrent of acts and policies, directives and memoranda, press releases and official explanations pour from the offices of government. They embrace topics of increasing specialization; requiring the general reporter and his editor to be a sanitation engineer on Monday, an educator by Wednesday, and an authority on the Sino-Soviet split by the end of the week.

These changes reflect on neither the motives nor the capacity of officials or press. They flow unavoidably from the growth of government and the complexities of the modern age.

It will take many years before we fully adjust to this immense expansion of our world, but certain simple and specific steps can be of help.

It should be possible, for example, to encourage freer contact between lower-level officials and the press. We are long past the time when a few men could fully comprehend the operations of government. In each department there are able men, specialists and experts, free from the tyranny of many political restraints, willing to devote time to detailed and serious exploration. Such fruitful cooperation is, of course, only possible if subordinates are free from fear of punishing reprisal when the inevitable indiscretion occurs.

Government officials could also help your task by reducing the number of briefings held on a background basis. It is often more out of lingering habit than necessity that the press is forbidden to mention the source of information intended for publication. The unfortunate consequence is the inability of an informed reader to make his own evaluation of the reliability, authority, and special interests of the official spokesman; forcing him to discount the news altogether or accept it on faith.

Much information which might illuminate issues and events is hidden in government agencies, not out of a desire for secrecy, but because its value as public information is never considered. We might well increase scrutiny of documents, cables, and reports, making public those which would increase understanding without jeopardizing the internal operations of government.

These issues of press freedom, national security and fair trial are not the artificial creation of heedless and hostile men anxious to damage the nation, impair justice, or limit liberty. They flow from the painful and necessary effort to adjust our institutions and habits of thought to changing values and a changing world. Never easy, the task is far more laborious when it engages the basic structures of our democracy. These problems, like our relationship itself, as both adversaries and allies, reflect the wise judgment of our Constitution to establish a necessary and fruitful tension between press and government; not for your sake or ours, but to enlarge the life of the nation.

Therefore, you serve the Republic, not as an instrument of authority or particular politics, but as the great mediator—not between government and people—but between the people and the most spacious possibilities of our society.

For once the obscuring turmoil of transient events and personal clash has lifted, we discover that our confidence in the press does not flow from your support or opposition, from admiration or from anger. It rests on those rooted and inviolable traditions which command you to help liberate the mind so citizens may approach the truths more closely; thus strengthening their resolve to exercise with pride and exuberant vitality their ultimate and rightful power over those of us in government, and over this city, and over all of you.

Those traditions and your duties are older than America itself. They spring from Andrew Hamilton's valiant and successful plea for the acquittal of newspaper editor John Peter Zenger in 1733. "It is not," he told the jury, "the cause of a poor printer . . . which you are trying. . . . It is the best cause; it is the cause of liberty . . . and by an impartial . . . verdict . . . [you will lay] a noble foundation for securing to ourselves [and] our posterity . . . that to which nature and the laws of our country have given us a right—the liberty of both exposing and opposing arbitrary power . . . by speaking and writing the truth."

UPON THE ACCEPTANCE OF THE 1967
WILLIAM ALLEN WHITE FOUNDATION AWARD
FOR JOURNALISTIC MERIT [3]

Wes Gallagher [4]

Among the current expressions enjoying wide favor is "credibility gap." Bill Moyers, former press secretary to President Johnson, remarked in a delightful speech on March 18, 1966, that the credibility gap was indeed a problem. "It is getting so bad we can't even believe our own leaks. There have been so many leaks we are stamping our morning newspapers 'TOP SECRET.'" Although applied largely to the alleged lack of frankness by government officials in providing necessary facts for the American people, the term has come to cover just about any lapse from candor. The suitor who doubts his girl friend's story on her whereabouts last evening tells her, in effect, and often with more pique than diplomacy, that her report falls short of credibility. The student who questions his instructor on a grade somewhat out of line with expectation, hints that the teacher's analysis of the facts is not satisfyingly believable. So credibility gaps are pointed out everywhere. But, after all, it is a mildly attractive expression, and plainly preferable to the harsher terms for which it euphemistically substitutes.

Though usually undeclared, a war of sorts does go on between persons who have facts they would rather not divulge, and those who do not have the information but want to report it. Accordingly, the press often points a finger at the government official for not providing exact data, and the official retaliates by saying the papers do not report the facts in proper perspective. Such a call for perspective reporting—especially of statistical measurements of unemployment, budgets, economic stability, and the like —was sounded by Secretary of Labor W. Willard Wirtz in an address before the Industrial Relations Research Association, meeting in San Francisco, on December 28, 1966.

A revealing analysis of perspective reporting appears in the speech by Wes Gallagher, reprinted below. A long-time reporter and now general manager of the Associated Press, Mr. Gallagher gave this address on February 10, 1967, at the University of Kansas on the occasion of his receiving the 1967 William Allen White Foundation Award for Journalistic Merit. Cited for his service and contributions to the profession and

[3] University of Kansas, Lawrence, February 10, 1967. Text furnished by Ann Whyte, secretary to Mr. Gallagher, with permission to reprint the address and Mr. Hugh Mulligan's reply.

[4] For biographical note, see Appendix.

his community, Mr. Gallagher responded with an appeal for perspective reporting—"the tool we need to use to keep the reader from associating a lack of credibility on the part of a news source with the medium that is carrying his statement." Indicating that the older methods of ordinary reporting were no longer adapted to the complexities of modern life, he asserted that "it is a rare case when one reporter can gather enough facts in a short time and come up with a story that will be authentic enough to convince and hold the attention of our new readers." Perspective reporting, on the other hand, enables a writer to present news "in its proper relationship to the whole and in relation to other news in its own time." It "dissects the situation today and compares it with the past." The flow of such news, Mr. Gallagher believed, influences the public. As an example of good perspective reporting, he cited a story by reporter Hugh Mulligan on the bombing flights over North Vietnam. Students may wish to compare the Mulligan report with some of the first-person stories of riding on bombing missions in World War II or Korea. A suitable report for comparative analysis is Edward R. Murrow's widely heralded "Orchestrated Hell," which was reprinted in REPRESENTATIVE AMERICAN SPEECHES: 1943-1944, pages 37-45.

Mr. Gallagher's speech moves along swiftly, is easy to read, and carries a considerable burden of thought with economy of style. It illustrates effectively what Dean Edward W. Barrett of the Columbia School of Journalism meant when he said the journalist should be possessed of an "art of expression that is lean, direct, precise, and deft."

I am happy to appear before such a literate and solvent audience. The solvency being demonstrated by the check that goes with this award.

The William Allen White Foundation award is one of the most outstanding in journalism. I am deeply honored—not only on my own behalf, but on behalf of the Associated Press as well—to be selected for this award.

When I started preparing this talk I planned to point out the difficulty of communication today by saying something like this:

"When man lived simply and primitively, the business of disseminating the news was done simply and primitively. But now in this complex civilization among people highly sophisticated, the job has become complex."

That's what I planned to say, but I found that William Allen White said exactly that in 1932, talking to journalism students at

Drake University. That makes him either thirty-five years ahead of his time or me thirty-five years behind.

But Mr. White lived in an age of relatively small government, and image-making was not the industry it is today. The problems of the journalist then, as Mr. White pointed out, were the same as they are today—to be the conscience of the public, the defender of its rights, its spokesman, its protector against malfeasance in government, and the people's voice whenever it needs to be heard.

All newsmen should make brief speeches, but before I begin to be brief . . . we'll have to go into some background.

First, the audience of the journalist today is quite different than even twenty years ago. Robert Ardrey, anthropologist and a playwright who wrote *African Genesis*, reflected on today's audience in his new book *The Territorial Imperative*. He said he has become aware that "a new human force—a force anonymous and unrecognized, informed and inquisitive, with allegiance to neither wealth nor poverty, to neither privilege nor petulance is silently appearing on earth and this class is massive."

"Informed and inquisitive"—these are the key words.

Statistically they are young—51 per cent under twenty-nine—and over 10 million are college graduates.

It is an impatient audience—too impatient to waste time on trivia. Deluged daily by the highly sophisticated techniques of Madison Avenue, it has become cynical and critical. It is eager for information but suspicious that it is being taken in by one device or another. It swallows up vast amounts of information and entertainment, but it hungers for the significant. It hungers for perspective. It hungers for understanding.

The audience is only half of the problem. The journalist stands between the audience and the sources of news. The sources of news have changed as much as the readers or listeners. First, the size and influence of government—local, state and Federal—have been enlarged enormously so they affect the lives of every individual in the world. Whether big government is good or bad is in political dispute, but big government seems inevitable. Republican or Democrat, Socialist or Conservative, the powers of government have constantly enlarged everywhere in the world. The sheer bulk has become a problem in itself.

The Agricultural Department employs 80,000 people, the State Department 43,000, Justice 33,000 and Defense 1,222,000. No individual citizen or group of citizens could begin to hope to find out what all those people are doing with the taxpayer's money on any given day, let alone year after year. Even trained reporters find it difficult to cope with such huge organizations.

The image-makers have been very busy in government. Press relations departments have grown even faster than other branches of government. We have reached the point where the Federal Government alone now spends scores of millions of dollars every year on sheer press agentry. The job of these press agents is to make disasters appear insignificant and molehills of success appear mountains of achievement.

Journalism's problems do not rest with government alone. The past three decades have seen an explosion of education and knowledge. The journalist of today, especially the specialist, must know a hundred times as much as his predecessor—just as the doctor of today must know a hundred times as much as the doctor of yesterday. Science has put spaceships around the moon, unleashed the demons of atomic weaponry, practically stamped out tuberculosis and infantile paralysis in the Western world. It has brought a higher standard of living for everyone and a greater chance of dying by violence.

Is it any wonder then that this vast new public looking at the huge apparatus of government and the contradictions of science is hard to satisfy?

The agitation of this society has been expressed in many ways.

"You can't believe what you read in the newspapers."

"There is a credibility gap in government."

"Television hides more than it shows."

"No politician ever tells the truth."

"All politicians are humbugs."

These are just a few of the phrases that you will hear daily. They are reflections of our time.

This society doubts the credibility of almost everything and is immune—if I can pronounce it—to humbugability.

And they have reasons for this attitude. In our time, the Vietnamese war has probably been the greatest contributor to the cynicism in this country. To cite a few examples of what they have heard:

"The war can only be won by the Vietnamese themselves and the United States will pull out more troops even if the war falters."

"Our responsibility is not to substitute ourselves for the Vietnamese but to train them to carry on the operation that they themselves are capable of."

Author—Secretary of Defense McNamara in 1963 and 1964. These are just a few of many such government statements made over five years of the war and proven wrong by events.

Within a week last fall, we had Secretary McNamara saying that the troop buildup in Vietnam would be slowed up and level off. Meanwhile, General Greene of the Marine Corps, in an off-the-record Tokyo press conference, said they would need 750,000 men in Vietnam. Senator Stennis set the figure needed at 600,000. Confusion multiplied!

The latest furor has been set off by the reporting of Harrison Salisbury of the New York *Times* and Bill Baggs of the Miami *News*. But the stage for Salisbury was set not by the New York *Times* but by the statements of United States Government officials during two years of bombing in North Vietnam. Assistant Secretary Arthur Sylvester recently challenged anyone to say that the Defense Department had ever claimed that "*all*" bombs fell only on military targets in North Vietnam. It is true that the Defense Department did not make an all-inclusive claim. But there was a concentrated effort on the part of every arm in government, including the Pentagon, to make it appear that the bombs fell only on military targets.

Questioned about the bombing accuracy in June of 1966, when the bombs were close to Hanoi and Haiphong, McNamara emphasized at a press conference that the pilots were carefully instructed to confine themselves to military targets. He said the pilots were told "not to destroy the Communist government of North Vietnam nor destroy or damage the people of North Vietnam."

A Pentagon spokesman said that the bombs fell "right on target."

McNamara added, "The pilots were especially briefed to avoid civilian areas. We have not hit Hanoi or Haiphong, we have hit oil storage facilities."

Senator Dirksen, a Republican who seems to echo the Administration, chimed in to say, "We are absolutely astounded at the real precision result."

On June 30, General Myers said that fuel dumps were hit by a "surgical type of treatment—this means holding civilian casualties to an absolute minimum and putting the bombs right on the money."

On the same day, Ambassador Goldberg said the bombings hit petroleum facilities "located away from the population center of Hanoi and Haiphong."

On July 1, Vice President Humphrey in Detroit said the raids were carried out "so as to avoid civilian casualties." July 2, an Administration spokesman said, "No more than one or two civilians—perhaps none—were killed in Wednesday's bombing of oil targets at Haiphong and Hanoi." The Administration spokesman said that this conclusion was based on aerial photographs of the raid. Just how such an exact count of civilian casualties could be deduced from photographs was not made clear, since the Administration first announced that 80 per cent of the oil facilities were hit, then revised this a few days later to 40 per cent to 50 per cent. Then on July 17, Secretary Cyrus Vance said that 66 per cent of the oil facilities had been destroyed.

Those aerial photographs seem to be the most flexible in history —they provided any kind of an answer a speaker wanted.

At any rate, the Administration's own attempt to convey the impression that bombs fell only on military targets set the stage for Salisbury's articles. He pointed out the inevitable—that bombs fall today, just as they did in World War II, on most any place—on

civilians and military installations alike, particularly if the bombings are heavy.

Flying at 600 or 1,000 miles an hour with only split seconds over
a target—shot at by ground fire and rockets and possibly attacked
by Migs—it is a wonder that the bombing is as accurate as it has
been. As a matter of fact, the bombings probably were more accurate than the statements about them.

How much different the picture would have been these past
two years if the Administration had said the bombs were directed
toward military targets but "inevitably some of them fell outside
the area and probably caused civilian casualties." Such repeated
statements would have been accurate, truthful and believed. And
Salisbury and Baggs' articles on the bombings would have not had
the world impact that they did.

In this continuing furor over the credibility gap, the reader associates the untrue statement of a public figure with the paper that
publishes it. This is like getting mad at the local editor because the
weatherman goofed. But it undoubtedly has a lot to do with public
disbelief of journalism.

There is a remedy for this I will come to shortly.

Some critics already believe journalism has lost its influence because of this lack of credibility.

But I don't think so. I don't think we have reached this point
because this vast audience *is* being influenced and *is* being influenced in such a way that it is still making the right judgments
as far as the world is concerned.

What influences this new class?

Scotty Reston, a resident Washington skeptic in his own right,
discussed in the magazine *Foreign Affairs* the influence of the journalist on diplomacy. He said, "The Lippmanns and Krocks have
followings, but news is more powerful than opinion."

I do not believe that an individual column, an individual edi-
torial, an individual television program influences to any significant degree this new sophisticated society.

But the *flow* of news does influence. If reporters in Vietnam
write day after day, as they did in the early sixties, that the war in

South Vietnam was going badly for the Vietnamese government, this is what the public believes. If today, the same hundreds and thousands of newspaper stories and broadcasts point out that militarily the war is at least a stalemate, this is what the public believes.

The flow of news, accurately reported, influences the public. And I stress *accurately*.

Facts presented logically have a ring of authenticity that over a period of time convince the vast majority of the reading and listening public regardless of their cynicism. There are still the extremists who believe nothing but their own preconceived ideas, but they are a small minority.

This does not mean the new "informed and inquisitive" public seeks to have heroes and villains clearly designated in the news. This more sophisticated class realizes that there are grays and various shades of gray in every situation. The trap the journalist must avoid is presenting a situation as black and white when the reader knows differently.

What tools do we need for our job? We have developed many and they have gone under different names—enterprise, reporting in depth, backgrounders. Now the emphasis should be on detailed "investigative reporting" and what I like to call it, "perspective reporting." Investigative reporting is certainly not new, but we cannot do investigative reporting as it was done a few years ago. Then the classic technique was to take a few facts and flail away at the malefactors editorially. Today's problems are much more complex and investigation of them takes a lot more time and effort. It is a rare case when one reporter can gather enough facts in a short time and come up with a story that will be authentic enough to convince and hold the attention of our new readers. Investigative reporting must be done with enough resources to match and overcome any obstacles—and there will be many. We can convince only by the most detailed presentation of facts, for facts alone have the ring of truth—opinion alone is useless.

Indicative of the resources that you need to throw into such a situation was the New York *Times* worldwide analysis of the operations of the CIA, which was months in preparation with scores of reporters working on various facets of it. In the same category was the Associated Press' own investigation into graft in Vietnam, which ran on virtually all front pages late last year. This story, too, was months in preparation. While the main burden was carried by two men, many others contributed to it over a period of time.

Investigative reporting is not the type you can hit just once and drop. You must come back again and again until the *flow* of news— the *flow of facts* if you want to put it that way—makes its impression on our new audience.

The other great weapon that we have is *perspective* reporting that can and must be used on the daily flow of news.

Perspective reporting is the tool we need to use to keep the reader from associating a lack of credibility on the part of a news source with the medium that is carrying his statement.

The dictionary defines perspective as "the art of depicting on a flat surface, various objects, architecture, landscape in such a way as to express its dimensions and its relation of parts one to the other and to the whole."

Perspective reporting is presenting news in its proper relationship to the whole and in relation to other news in its own time.

Perspective reporting dissects the situation today and compares it with the past.

For example, in doing an article today on General de Gaulle, do you portray only the man who has been raiding our gold supply, throwing our troops out of France, keeping Great Britain out of the Common Market, attacking our policy on Vietnam? Or do you put this complex man in perspective with the hero de Gaulle of the forties, who rallied France, saved it in the postwar years and then came back again a decade later to save France from anarchy?

Perspective reporting sees both men and evaluates both for the reader. It presents a complete picture. It is cool. Much cooler and objective than the former Secretary of State I met in Washington some months ago and asked if he felt General de Gaulle had ever been right on a single political question.

"Never," he replied looking me straight in the eye, and he wasn't joking.

Trying to put one man, even a General de Gaulle, in perspective is a simple problem compared with writing about the emotional problems today such as integration and segregation, China versus Russia or for that matter China versus China.

Perspective reporting requires a cold, logical approach to the news. It requires dogged pursuit of facts until the writer is convinced that he has everything he can possibly dig out. The facts must then be sorted and logically presented, devoid of conclusion-jumping or emotionalism.

If these precepts are followed, the reader—no matter how cynical or sophisticated—will find himself convinced. The article will have that feel of authenticity.

Perspective reporting can and should be used everywhere, not just on complicated situations.

Recently our Hugh Mulligan had a long story on just how pilots felt in flying and bombing over North Vietnam. It was a fascinating article—many times better than those first-person stories of riding on bombing missions in World War II or Korea. I had given orders to the Saigon staff that the day of the reporter flying on bombing missions had been overdone since World War II, and I certainly didn't want anyone flying over North Vietnam, no matter what the opportunity was. Hugh's story had so much detail and such a feeling of participation that, in reading it, I became disturbed he perhaps had violated this order. So I wrote him a letter, and this is what he wrote in reply.

No, I didn't go, but neither did I get all that detail just by interviewing. Would you believe that the original story was twice as long? I have no complaints against my editors—whoever cut it in half did a superior job.

Mulligan went on to say:

The point is that you don't get that kind of detail just from interviews. I lived with these guys in their barracks for almost a week, went to the movies with them, ate with them. It took me four days to find a communicative guy like Greene. On the day of the flight, I got up with them, attended all the top secret briefings, rode out to the flight line, watched the pre-flight, went by jeep to the armament pit, then to the runway control point. I watched them take off, waited on the strip, Ann Sheridan-style, until they returned a half an hour, hour or so later. I talked with the crew chiefs, attended all the top-secret briefings and then got Randy and Duff to tell me in simple English, minute by minute, exactly what happened. We did it over a beer at the officers' club. Then I wrote, discarded and wrote until I had it all in. Sometime you may be interested in reading all the details.

That is how Mulligan got his story.

I think this illustrates the difference between ordinary reporting and perspective reporting. Mulligan took a week or ten days to get his carefully detailed account of a pilot's experiences over North Vietnam. I cannot remember any reporter, including myself, who spent more than a few hours in World War II on similar stories. Mulligan did a far better reporting job. When you read his story you felt you were sitting right behind the pilot in a way that no story from previous wars made you feel.

Everything Mulligan presented was true and was in relation to other facts and to the whole mission—this was perspective reporting. There could be no doubt in the reader's mind that this was the way it happened.

It is not always as easy to get the facts as it is in this particular type of war reporting. But by the relatively simple device of admitting that we failed to get the facts in a certain situation, or that a public official refused to comment on a critical point, we can convey authenticity to the reader. Most reporters hesitate to put such phrases into their stories, but when they leave gaps unanswered, their stories are not believed.

The Government, too, would be far better off if, in advocating its programs, it admitted failures from time to time. This, too, would give the reader more confidence in the credibility of what is being said.

Every day I see stories—by AP as well as others—where the reporter accepted statements without question and didn't go deep enough or ask enough questions—perhaps embarrassing questions—to obtain the real perspective. You may say that only an editor would realize that these are missing, but if you do you misjudge our new society—"informed and inquisitive with allegiance to neither wealth nor poverty nor privilege nor petulance."

There is no doubt the flow of news can and does influence the most sophisticated critic. Even the most violent doubter must take his arguments from the news itself.

If we, as journalists, use the tools we have at our disposal to put the news in perspective, then the news will have that ring of authenticity, and we won't have to fear any credibility gap. Nor will the lack of credibility of some news sources rub off on the journalist.

The public will have confidence in the journalist not only as a conveyer of vital information, but as the principal guardian of its freedoms as well.

A SEARCH FOR EQUITY

ADDRESS BEFORE THE AMERICAN SOCIETY OF NEWSPAPER EDITORS [1]

Robert S. McNamara [2]

With the exception of the Vietnam war, few subjects provoke more spirited concern in classroom discussions than the draft. Among the disputants, the range of views on this explosively controversial topic is wide, running all the way from a sort of angered acceptance of the seemingly inevitable to an impassioned outrage at its apparent inequity. The standards for deferment are questioned; the method of selection is condemned. Throughout much of the debate runs the persistent theme "It's not fair," reflecting the philosophy of the Orwellian state in which all are equal but some are more equal than their brothers.

Ralph Waldo Emerson once observed that "nothing is fair or good alone." But it is the job of thoughtful men, in and out of government, to work unstintingly at hammering out a kind of rough justice, consistent with national requirements, and especially where family ties, training careers, and even life itself are at stake. The debates and campus protests reflect the understandable concerns of today's youth; and the older generation has an obligation to help mobilize these yearnings into satisfying and useful work.

During recent months the Administration has taken a close look at the present Selective Service System. While the increased concern over the draft did not originate with it, Secretary of Defense Robert S. McNamara's speech in Montreal, Canada, on May 18, 1966, before the American Society of Newspaper Editors, did give effective impetus to the dialogue. This came as a surprise to many who view the Secretary of Defense, an uncommonly influential man in Washington, as a cold, methodical administrator who deals only in pinpoint calculations. But, according to James Reston, Mr. McNamara is a "philosophical computer and the philosopher in him is stronger than the computer." Accordingly, he "said what he believed . . . and concentrated on what he thought should be instead of what actually is at the present time." Mr. McNamara in effect challenged the conventional assumption that purely military ingredients create security; and he

[1] Montreal, Canada, May 18, 1966. Text furnished by Peter A. Erickson, Directorate for Information Services, United States Department of Defense, with permission for this reprint.

[2] For biographical note, see Appendix.

cited the relationship between Canada and the United States to confirm the belief. These two countries "are at peace for reasons that have nothing whatever to do with our mutual military readiness."

He asserted that America's role in world affairs requires that we help provide security to the newly developed nations. And one of the less understood categories of assistance is training in *civic action*. This theme, linked with his categorical assertion that the present Selective Service System is an inequity because it draws on only a minority of young men, has evoked much controversy. He called for a plan which would require "every young person in the United States to give two years of service to his country—whether in one of the military services, in the Peace Corps, or in some other volunteer developmental work at home or abroad." While the details of the plan were a little nebulous, it was generally interpreted as a call for universal national service, though perhaps not on a compulsory basis. It was likened to the Peace Corps, which Harris Wofford, its associate director, has called "a university in dispersion." Some were reminded of William James' essay "The Moral Equivalent of War" in which he urged an "army" of youth "enlisted against nature" in a work program.

Since the delivery of Mr. McNamara's speech, major recommendations for a change in the draft have come from Washington. On February 27, 1967, a study commission appointed by the House Armed Services Committee endorsed generally the present Selective Service System but recommended that the youngest men, classified 1-A in the nineteen- and twenty-year brackets, be inducted first. On March 4, the National Advisory Commission on Selective Service issued its report. It also recommended, among other things, that the youngest be called first; that student deferments should "never be allowed to become, in effect, exemptions"; and that the draft be determined by lot—what the *New Republic* has called "a computerized fish bowl which would randomly select draftees." On March 6, the President announced that unless Congress prevents the order, he will set up by January 1, 1969, some sort of lottery for selecting the men for military service.

Thus the lines are drawn for an important debate in which the issues of student deferment, selection by lottery, and priority of draft call according to age will doubtless be crucial.

Any American would be fortunate to visit this lovely island city, in this hospitable land.

But there is a special satisfaction for a Secretary of Defense to cross the longest border in the world—and realize that it is also the least armed border in the world. It prompts one to reflect how negative and narrow a notion of defense still clouds our century.

There is still among us an almost ineradicable tendency to think of our *security* problem as being exclusively a *military* problem—and to think of the military problem as being exclusively a *weapons-system* or hardware problem.

The plain, blunt truth is that contemporary man still conceives of war and peace in much the same stereotyped terms that his ancestors did. The fact that these ancestors—both recent and remote—were conspicuously unsuccessful at avoiding war, and enlarging peace, doesn't seem to dampen our capacity for clichés.

We still tend to conceive of national security almost solely as a state of armed readiness: a vast, awesome arsenal of weaponry.

We still tend to assume that it is primarily this purely military ingredient that creates security.

We are still haunted by this concept of military hardware.

But how limited a concept this actually is, becomes apparent when one ponders the kind of peace that exists between the United States and Canada.

It is a very cogent example. Here we are, two modern nations: highly developed technologically, each with immense territory, both enriched with great reserves of natural resources, each militarily sophisticated—and yet, we sit across from one another, divided by an unguarded frontier of thousands of miles . . . and there is not a remotest set of circumstances, in any imaginable time-frame of the future, in which our two nations would wage war on one another.

It is so unthinkable an idea as to be totally absurd.

But *why* is that so?

Is it because we are both ready in an instant to hurl our military hardware at one another?

Is it because we are both zeroed in on one another's vital targets?

Is it because we are both armed to our technological teeth that we do not go to war?

The whole notion—as applied to our two countries—is ludicrous.

Canada and the United States are at peace for reasons that have nothing whatever to do with our mutual military readiness.

We are at peace—truly at peace—because of the vast fund of compatible beliefs, common principles, and shared ideals.

We have our differences and our diversity—and let us hope for the sake of a mutually rewarding relationship we never become sterile carbon copies of one another.

But the whole point is that our basis of mutual peace has nothing whatever to do with our military hardware.

Now this is not to say, obviously enough, that the concept of military deterrence is no longer relevant in the contemporary world.

Unhappily, it still is critically relevant with respect to our potential adversaries.

But it has no relevance whatever between the United States and Canada.

We are not adversaries. We are not going to become adversaries. And it is not mutual military deterrence that keeps us from becoming adversaries. It is mutual respect for common principles.

Now I mention this—as obvious as it all is—simply as a kind of *reductio ad absurdum* of the concept that military hardware is the exclusive or even the primary ingredient of permanent peace in the mid-twentieth century.

In the United States—over the past five years—we have achieved a considerably improved balance in our total military posture. That was the mandate I received from Presidents Kennedy and Johnson; and with their support, and that of the Congress, we have been able to create a strengthened force structure of land, sea, and air components—with a vast increase in mobility and materiel—and with a massive superiority in nuclear retaliatory power over any combination of potential adversaries.

Our capabilities for nuclear, conventional, and countersubversive war have all been broadened and improved; and we have accomplished this through military budgets that were in fact lesser percentages of our gross national product than in the past.

From the point of view of combat readiness, the United States has never been militarily stronger.

We intend to maintain that readiness.

But if we think profoundly about the matter, it is clear that this purely military posture is not the central element in our security.

A nation can reach the point at which it does not buy more security for itself simply by buying more military hardware—we are at that point.

The decisive factor for a powerful nation—already adequately armed—is the *character of its relationships with the world.*

In this respect, there are three broad groups of nations: first, those that are struggling to develop; secondly, those free nations that have reached a level of strength and prosperity that enables them to contribute to the peace of the world; and finally, those nations who might be tempted to make themselves our adversaries.

For each of these groups, the United States—to preserve its own intrinsic security—has to have distinctive sets of relationships.

First, we have to help protect those developing countries which genuinely need and request our help, and which—as an essential precondition—are willing and able to help themselves.

Second, we have to encourage and achieve a more effective partnership with those nations who can and should share international peace-keeping responsibilities.

Third, we must do all we realistically can to reduce the risk of conflict with those who might be tempted to take up arms against us.

Let us examine these three sets of relationships in detail.

First, the developing nations.

Roughly one hundred countries today are caught up in the difficult transition from traditional to modern societies.

There is no uniform rate of progress among them, and they range from primitive mosaic societies—fractured by tribalism and held feebly together by the slenderest of political sinews—to relatively sophisticated countries, well on the road to agricultural sufficiency and industrial competence.

This sweeping surge of development, particularly across the whole southern half of the globe, has no parallel in history.

It has turned traditionally listless areas of the world into seething cauldrons of change.

On the whole, it has not been a very peaceful process.

In the last eight years alone there have been no less than 164 internationally significant outbreaks of violence—each of them specifically designed as a serious challenge to the authority, or the very existence, of the government in question.

Eighty-two different governments have been directly involved.

What is striking is that only 15 of these 164 significant resorts to violence have been military conflicts between two states.

And not a single one of the 164 conflicts has been a formally declared war.

Indeed, there has not been a formal declaration of war—anywhere in the world—since World War II.

The planet is becoming a more dangerous place to live on—not merely because of a potential nuclear holocaust—but also because of the large number of *de facto* conflicts and because the trend of such conflicts is growing rather than diminishing.

At the beginning of 1958, there were 23 prolonged insurgencies going on about the world. As of February 1, 1966, there were 40.

Further, the total number of outbreaks of violence has increased each year: in 1958, there were 34; in 1965, there were 58.

But what is most significant of all is that there is a direct and constant relationship between the incidence of violence and the economic status of the countries afflicted.

The World Bank divides nations, on the basis of per capita income, into four categories: rich, middle-income, poor, and very poor.

The rich nations are those with a per capita income of $750 per year or more. The current United States level is more than $2700. There are 27 of these rich nations. They possess 75 per cent of the world's wealth, though roughly only 25 per cent of the world's population.

Since 1958, only *one* of these 27 nations has suffered a major internal upheaval on its own territory.

But observe what happens at the other end of the economic scale. Among the 38 very poor nations—those with a per capita income of under $100 a year—no less than 32 have suffered significant conflicts. Indeed, they have suffered an average of two major outbreaks of violence per country in the eight-year period. That is a great deal of conflict.

What is worse, it has been, predominantly, conflict of a prolonged nature.

The trend holds predictably constant in the case of the two other categories: the poor, and the middle-income nations. Since 1958, 87 per cent of the very poor nations, 69 per cent of the poor nations, and 48 per cent of the middle-income nations have suffered serious violence.

There can, then, be no question but that there is an irrefutable relationship between violence and economic backwardness. And the trend of such violence is up, not down.

Now, it would perhaps be somewhat reassuring if the gap between the rich nations and the poor nations were closing; and economic backwardness were significantly receding.

But it is not. The economic gap is widening.

By the year 1970, over one half of the world's total population will live in the independent nations sweeping across the southern half of the planet. But this hungering half of the human race will by then command only one sixth of the world's total of goods and services.

By the year 1975, the dependent children of these nations alone —children under fifteen years of age—will equal the *total* population of the developed nations to the north.

Even in our own abundant societies, we have reason enough to worry over the tensions that coil and tighten among underprivileged young people, and finally flail out in delinquency and crime. What are we to expect from a whole hemisphere of youth where mounting frustrations are likely to fester into eruptions of violence and extremism?

Annual per capita income in roughly half of the 80 underdeveloped nations that are members of the World Bank is rising by a paltry 1 per cent a year or less. By the end of the century, these nations—at their present rates of growth—will reach a per capita income of barely $170 a year. The United States, by the same criteria, will attain a per capita income of $4,500.

The conclusion to all of this is blunt and inescapable: given the certain connection between economic stagnation and the incidence of violence, the years that lie ahead for the nations in the southern half of the globe are pregnant with violence.

This would be true even if no threat of Communist subversion existed—as it clearly does.

Both Moscow and Peking—however harsh their internal differences—regard the whole modernization process as an ideal environment for the growth of communism. Their experience with subversive internal war is extensive; and they have developed a considerable array of both doctrine and practical measures in the art of political violence.

What is often misunderstood is that Communists are capable of subverting, manipulating, and finally directing for their own ends the wholly legitimate grievances of a developing society.

But it would be a gross oversimplification to regard communism as the central factor in every conflict throughout the underdeveloped world. Of the 149 serious internal insurgencies in the past eight years, Communists have been involved in only 58 of them—38 per cent of the total—and this includes seven instances in which a Communist regime itself was the target of the uprising.

Whether Communists are involved or not, violence anywhere in a taut world transmits sharp signals through the complex ganglia of international relations; and the security of the United States *is* related to the security and stability of nations half a globe away.

But neither conscience nor sanity itself suggests that the United States is, should, or could be the Global Gendarme.

Quite the contrary, experience confirms what human nature suggests: that in most instances of internal violence, the local people themselves are best able to deal directly with the situation within the framework of their own traditions.

The United States has no mandate from on high to police the world, and no inclination to do so. There have been classic cases in which our deliberate non-action was the wisest action of all.

Where our help is not sought, it is seldom prudent to volunteer.

Certainly we have no charter to rescue floundering regimes, who have brought violence on themselves by deliberately refusing to meet the legitimate expectations of their citizenry.

Further, throughout the next decade advancing technology will reduce the requirement for bases and staging rights at particular locations abroad, and the whole pattern of forward deployment will gradually change.

But—though all these *caveats* are clear enough—the irreducible fact remains that our security is related directly to the security of the newly developing world.

And our role must be precisely this: to help provide security to those developing nations which genuinely need and request our help, and which demonstrably are willing and able to help themselves.

The rub comes in this: we do not always grasp the meaning of the word *security* in this context.

In a modernizing society, security means development.

Security is *not* military hardware—though it may include it. Security is *not* military force—though it may involve it. Security is *not* traditional military activity—though it may encompass it.

Security *is* development.

Without development, there can be no security.

A developing nation that does not in fact develop simply *cannot* remain "secure."

It cannot remain secure for the intractable reason that its own citizenry cannot shed its human nature.

If security implies anything, it implies a minimal measure of order and stability.

Without internal development of at least a minimal degree, order and stability are simply not possible. They are not possible because human nature cannot be frustrated beyond intrinsic limits. It reacts—because it *must*.

Now, that is what we do not always understand; and that is also what governments of modernizing nations do not always understand.

But by emphasizing that security arises from development, I do not say that an underdeveloped nation cannot be subverted from within; or be aggressed upon from without; or be the victim of a combination of the two.

It can. And to prevent any or all of these conditions, a nation does require appropriate military capabilities to deal with the specific problem. But the specific *military* problem is only a narrow facet of the broader security problem.

Military force can help provide law and order—but only to the degree that a basis for law and order already exists in the developing society: a basic willingness on the part of the people to cooperate.

The law and order is a shield, behind which the central fact of security—development—can be achieved.

Now we are not playing a semantic game with these words.

The trouble is that we have been lost in a semantic jungle for too long. We have come to identify "security" with exclusively military phenomena; and most particularly with military hardware.

But it just isn't so. And we need to accommodate to the facts of the matter, if we want to see security survive and grow in the southern half of the globe.

Development means economic, social, and political progress. It means a reasonable standard of living—and the word "reasonable" in this context requires continual redefinition. What is "reasonable" in an earlier stage of development will become "unreasonable" in a later stage.

As development progresses, security progresses; and when the people of a nation have organized their own human and natural resources to provide themselves with what they need and expect out of life—and have learned to compromise peacefully among competing demands in the larger national interest—then, their resistance to disorder and violence will be enormously increased.

Conversely, the tragic need of desperate men to resort to force to achieve the inner imperatives of human decency will diminish.

Now, I have said that the role of the United States is to help provide security to these modernizing nations—provided they need and request our help; and are clearly willing and able to help themselves.

But what should our help be?

Clearly, it should be help towards development. In the military sphere, that involves two broad categories of assistance.

We should help the developing nation with such training and equipment as is necessary to maintain the protective shield behind which development can go forward.

The dimensions of that shield vary from country to country; but what is essential is that it should be a shield, and *not* a capacity for external aggression.

The second—and perhaps less understood category of military assistance in a modernizing nation—is training in civic action.

"Civic action" is another one of those semantic puzzles. Too few Americans—and too few officials in developing nations—really comprehend what military civic action means.

Essentially, it means using indigenous military forces for non-traditional military projects—projects that are useful to the local population in fields such as education, public works, health, sanitation, agriculture—indeed, anything connected with economic or social progress.

It has had some impressive results. In the past four years, the United States assisted civic action program, worldwide, has constructed or repaired more than ten thousand miles of roads; built over one thousand schools; hundreds of hospitals and clinics; and has provided medical and dental care to approximately four million people.

What is important is that all this was done by indigenous men in uniform. Quite apart from the developmental projects themselves, the program powerfully alters the negative image of the military man, as the oppressive preserver of the stagnant status quo.

But assistance in the purely military sphere is not enough. Economic assistance is also essential. The President is determined that our aid should be hard-headed and rigorously realistic: that it should deal directly with the *roots* of underdevelopment, and not merely attempt to alleviate the symptoms. His bedrock principle is that United States economic aid—no matter what its magnitude —is futile unless the country in question is resolute in making the primary effort itself. That will be the criterion, and that will be the crucial condition for all our future assistance.

Only the developing nations themselves can take the fundamental measures that make outside assistance meaningful. These measures are often unpalatable—and frequently call for political courage and decisiveness. But to fail to undertake painful, but essential, reform inevitably leads to far more painful revolutionary violence. Our economic assistance is designed to offer a reasonable alternative to that violence. It is designed to help substitute peaceful progress for tragic internal conflict.

The United States intends to be compassionate and generous in this effort, but it is not an effort it can carry exclusively by itself. And thus it looks to those nations who have reached the point of self-sustaining prosperity to increase *their* contribution to the development—and, thus, to the security—of the modernizing world.

And that brings me to the second set of relationships that I underscored at the outset; it is the policy of the United States to encourage and achieve a more effective partnership with those nations who can, and should, share international peace-keeping responsibilities.

America has devoted a higher proportion of its gross national product to its military establishment than any other major free world nation. This was true even before our increased expenditures in Southeast Asia.

We have had, over the last few years, as many men in uniform as all the nations of Western Europe combined—even though they have a population half again greater than our own.

Now, the American people are not going to shirk their obligations in any part of the world, but they clearly cannot be expected to bear a disproportionate share of the common burden indefinitely.

If, for example, other nations genuinely believe—as they say they do—that it is in the common interest to deter the expansion of Red China's economic and political control beyond its national boundaries, then they must take a more active role in guarding the defense perimeter.

Let me be perfectly clear: this is not to question the policy of neutralism or nonalignment of any particular nation. But it is to emphasize that the independence of such nations can—in the end— be fully safeguarded only by collective agreements among themselves and their neighbors.

The plain truth is the day is coming when no single nation, however powerful, can undertake *by itself* to keep the peace outside its own borders. Regional and international organizations for peace-keeping purposes are as yet rudimentary; but they must grow in experience and be strengthened by deliberate and practical co-operative action.

In this matter, the example of Canada is a model for nations everywhere. As Prime Minister Pearson pointed out eloquently in New York just last week: Canada

is as deeply involved in the world's affairs as any country of its size. We accept this because we have learned over fifty years that isolation from the policies that determine war does not give us immunity from the bloody, sacrificial consequences of their failure. We learned that in 1914 and again in 1939. . . . That is why we have been proud to send our men to take part in every peace-keeping operation of the United Nations—in Korea, and Kashmir, and the Suez, and the Congo, and Cyprus.

The Organization of the American States in the Dominican Republic, the more than thirty nations contributing troops or supplies to assist the Government of South Vietnam, indeed even the parallel efforts of the United States and the Soviet Union in the Pakistan-India conflict—these efforts, together with those of the UN, are the first attempts to substitute multinational for unilateral policing of violence. They point to the peace-keeping patterns of the future.

We must not merely applaud the idea. We must dedicate talent, resources, and hard practical thinking to its implementation.

In Western Europe—an area whose burgeoning economic vi-tality stands as a monument to the wisdom of the Marshall Plan— the problems of security are neither static nor wholly new. Fundamental changes are under way, though certain inescapable realities remain.

The conventional forces of NATO, for example, still require a nuclear backdrop far beyond the capability of any Western European nation to supply, and the United States is fully committed to provide that major nuclear deterrent.

However, the European members of the Alliance have a natural desire to participate more actively in nuclear planning. A central task of the Alliance today is, therefore, to work out the relationships and institutions through which shared nuclear planning can be effective. We have made a practical and promising start in the Special Committee of NATO Defense Ministers.

Common planning and consultation are essential aspects of any sensible substitute to the unworkable and dangerous alternative of independent national nuclear forces within the Alliance.

And even beyond the Alliance, we must find the means to prevent the proliferation of nuclear weapons. That is a clear imperative.

There are, of course, risks in nonproliferation arrangements; but they cannot be compared with the infinitely greater risks that would arise out of the increase in national nuclear stockpiles.

In the calculus of risk, to proliferate independent national nuclear forces is not a mere arithmetical *addition* of danger. We would not be merely adding up risks. We would be insanely *multiplying* them.

If we seriously intend to pass on a world to our children that is not threatened by nuclear holocaust, we must come to grips with the problem of proliferation.

A reasonable nonproliferation agreement is feasible. For there is *no* adversary with whom we do not share a common interest in avoiding mutual destruction triggered by an irresponsible nth power.

That brings me to the third and last set of relationships the United States must deal with: Those with nations who might be tempted to take up arms against us.

These relationships call for realism. But realism is not a hardened, inflexible, unimaginative attitude. The realistic mind is a restlessly creative mind—free of naïve delusions, but full of practical alternatives.

There *are* practical alternatives to our current relationships with both the Soviet Union and Communist China.

A vast ideological chasm separates us from them—and to a degree, separates them from one another.

There is nothing to be gained from our seeking an ideological rapprochement; but breaching the isolation of great nations like Red China, even when that isolation is largely of its own making, reduces the danger of potentially catastrophic misunderstandings, and increases the incentive on both sides to resolve disputes by reason rather than by force.

There are many ways in which we can build bridges toward nations who would cut themselves off from meaningful contact with us. We can do so with properly balanced trade relations, diplomatic contacts, and in some cases even by exchanges of military observers.

We have to know where it is we want to place this bridge; what sort of traffic we want to travel over it; and on what mutual foundations the whole structure can be designed.

There are no one-cliff bridges. If you are going to span a chasm, you have to rest the structure on both cliffs.

Now cliffs, generally speaking, are rather hazardous places. Some people are afraid even to look over the edge. But in a thermonuclear world, we cannot afford any political acrophobia.

President Johnson has put the matter squarely. By building bridges to those who make themselves our adversaries "we can help gradually to create a community of interest, a community of trust, and a community of effort."

With respect to a "community of effort" let me suggest a concrete proposal for our own present young generation in the United States.

It is a committed and dedicated generation: it has proven that in its enormously impressive performance in the Peace Corps overseas; and in its willingness to volunteer for a final assault on such poverty and lack of opportunity that still remain in our own country.

As matters stand, our present Selective Service System draws on only a minority of eligible young men.

That is an inequity.

It seems to me that we could move toward remedying that inequity by asking every young person in the United States to give two years of service to his country—whether in one of the military services, in the Peace Corps, or in some other volunteer developmental work at home or abroad.

We could encourage other countries to do the same; and we could work out exchange programs—much as the Peace Corps is already planning to do.

While this is not an altogether new suggestion, it has been criticized as inappropriate while we are engaged in a shooting war.

But I believe precisely the opposite is the case. It is more appropriate now than ever. For it would underscore what our whole purpose is in Vietnam—and indeed anywhere in the world where coercion, or injustice, or lack of decent opportunity still holds sway.

It would make meaningful the central concept of security: a world of decency and development—where every man can feel that his personal horizon is rimmed with hope.

Mutual interest—mutual trust—mutual effort; those are the goals. Can we achieve those goals with the Soviet Union, and with Communist China? Can they achieve them with one another?

The answer to these questions lies in the answer to an even more fundamental question.

Who is man?

Is he a rational animal?

If he is, then the goals can ultimately be achieved.

If he is not, then there is little point in making the effort.

All the evidence of history suggests that man is indeed a rational animal—but with a near infinite capacity for folly. His history seems largely a halting, but persistent, effort to raise his reason above his animality.

He draws blueprints for Utopia. But never quite gets it built. In the end, he plugs away obstinately with the only building material really ever at hand: his own part-comic, part-tragic, part-cussed, but part-glorious nature.

I, for one, would not count a global free society out.

Coercion, after all, merely captures man.

Freedom captivates him.

ADDRESS AT THE CATHOLIC UNIVERSITY OF AMERICA [3]

W. WILLARD WIRTZ [4]

Proposals for the establishment of national service plans—fashioned roughly after the Peace Corps, VISTA (Volunteers in Service to America), and others—have been discussed widely during the past year. The proponents view such programs as stimulators of youthful morale and extensions of the helping hand, both at home and in the underdeveloped lands. All inquiries into such suggestions have, however, run head-on into difficult questions: Shall the service, possibly for both men and women in the eighteen-twenty-six-year bracket, be compulsory? How can it be equated with the military program? Is it to be regarded as an alternative to military duty? The Report of the National Advisory Commission on Selective Service, released in March 1967, concluded that a system of universal training is designed largely "to offer physical fitness, self-discipline and remedial training to great numbers of young Americans" and that it is not a substitute for the draft. Hence, it "cannot be justified on the grounds of military need." As for "volunteer national service as an alternative to military service," the Commission saw no fair way to equate the two programs.

Secretary of Labor W. Willard Wirtz used the military draft as the springboard for his talk on November 16, 1966, before the students and faculty of the Catholic University of America in Washington, D.C. Adapting his remarks skillfully to the young people in the audience, he spoke of a broad policy for youth which would correct inequities fully as haphazard and serious as those involved in the selection for military service. Regarding unfairness in the latter program, he asked: "Is it worse than the unfairness of the way one boy out of every two gets to college and the other one doesn't?" "Whatever this country's need may be for a fair and effective method of distributing the obligation of some young men to fight," he went on, "it is only a small part of the infinitely larger and encompassing need for a fair and effective method of distributing the opportunity for all young men and women to learn, to work, to serve all the nation's and the world's needs, and to make sense out of their lives." Accordingly, he suggested a youth policy that would link opportunity with responsibility and prepare all young people for "useful lifetime membership" in the community.

[3] Washington, D.C., November 16, 1966. Text furnished by John W. Leslie, Director, Office of Information, United States Department of Labor, with permission for this reprint.

[4] For biographical note, see Appendix.

Former professor of law at the State University of Iowa and at Northwestern University, Mr. Wirtz is a polished speaker, with a fine sense of humor, and a strong, direct delivery. A. H. Raskin of the New York *Times* has referred to his "clinical precision in the use of words." A delightful piece by Mr. Wirtz, mentioned previously in the headnote to Wes Gallagher's speech (page 148 of this volume), deserves a second reference. In that address, before the Industrial Relations Research Association on December 28, 1966, Secretary Wirtz spoke of having to listen "to an unwanted amount of other people's public speaking which occasionally gets in the way of my own." And he referred to his "habit of jotting down, instead of the speaker's monumental message, his minumental metaphors —the little slips of the tongue every speaker makes when he gets as tired as his audience was from the beginning."

Thereupon followed, with appropriate footnotes, specimens of gnarled rhetoric and distressed metaphors which he had gleefully harvested. The collection proves indeed that he has—to use one of the specimens from his list—kept his "ear to the grindstone recently."

These remarks were announced last week by *Tower* as being "on current problems connected with labor."

That should probably have settled it. *Tower* has just received, once again, the Associated Collegiate Press All-American award. Furthermore, any change of this subject now will undoubtedly be construed as widening the credibility gap the press finds opening up between the Administration and the fourth estate. Finally, I admit that if I had been writing that *Tower* story last week instead of this speech last night I would have written it exactly that way.

This seems to me, nevertheless, to carry freedom of the press too far. For the fact is that *Tower* failed, in its reporting, to consult the world's leading, indeed only, living authority on my thoughts for tonight. Furthermore, some informal checking I have had done discloses that "current problems connected with labor" are so far down the list of matters of interest to CU students that they hardly show up at all, and I am surprised any of you did.

When I asked what does occupy campus attention today I was told that the principal subject of discussion—except for an old perennial regarding which I profess continuing interest but no special knowledge—is "the draft"; and there was strong suggestion that these remarks be built around that subject.

This presented another difficulty. The matter of the draft is presently being considered by the National Commission on Selective Service, appointed by President Johnson. Until the Commission makes its report in January, any detailed comment of mine regarding this subject would be inappropriate.

But a deadline is the father of invention. I propose to take "the draft" only as a starting point for the discussion of a related and broader area in which I think your reported interests and my own official concerns coincide at least a little.

There is the exciting possibility that the interest which has now been aroused in eliminating unfairness from the system of selecting young men for military service will lead to responsible action regarding the infinitely broader unfairness of a whole system—or lack of system—by which young men and women alike are selected in this country for *all kinds* of service—and education—and opportunity.

Not to be unpleasant, but to be specific, let me put the point in personal terms: By being here, the students of this University are the beneficiaries of a selective system more haphazard and inequitable than any method yet tried or suggested for selection for military service.

You complain, properly in my judgment, of the unfairness of the method by which one boy out of every two is selected for some kind of military service. But is it worse than the unfairness of the way one boy or girl out of every two gets to college and the other one doesn't? Consider the fact that a higher proportion of those in the lower half of their high school class who enjoy the accident of well-to-do parents go to college than is true of those in the upper half of the class whose accident was that they were created equal but to poorer parentage.

The question of whether the value of a college education is least diminished by military interruption before or during or after it isn't very important in a family to whom that value is completely denied.

I received recently, because of my responsibility for establishing occupational deferments from the draft, a proposal that all boys in apprenticeship programs—in the building trades, for example—be given deferred status. The not inconsiderable argument made for it was that apprenticeship is the poorer boy's college.

Neither a military service lottery nor any deferment system is as serious an affront to American principle as the game of bingo a dropout has to play when he, or she, fills out the blanks on an employment application form: Race? Sex? Highest grade reached in school? Skills? Previous employment? Why did you leave?

Whatever this country's need may be for a fair and effective method of distributing the obligation of some young men to fight, it is only a small part of the infinitely larger and encompassing need for a fair and effective method of distributing the opportunity for all young men and women to learn, to work, to serve all the nation's and the world's needs, and to make sense out of their own lives.

I want to make it clear that these remarks are not going to be limited to a plea for equity of opportunity. If I read the current national mood, and guess at your own reaction, it is that there has been too little done about people's not *using* the opportunity they already have.

I suggest that there are three essential elements in a rational, equitable and effective "policy for youth."

> *First,* that it be required that every boy and girl "register in" with the community when he or she reaches age eighteen.
>
> *Second,* that it be recognized as the community's obligation to provide every youth with the *opportunity* to receive at that point two years of further education, occupational training, a chance to participate in a service program, or a job.
>
> *Third,* that it be recognized as the youth's obligation, in return, to *use* this opportunity.

Now in more detail:

There is as much reason, and more, to require every American youth to "register" for living as for fighting. We need, as Point I in a policy for youth, a procedure for making meaningful contact between each individual and the community at the point at which the individual comes up to what is in most cases the critically formative stage in his, or her, career.

Suppose there were established in each community, as part of a national system, an Opportunity Board—made up of the community's outstanding educator, doctor, minister, business man, labor leader, and two representatives of those in the community aged sixteen to twenty-one, selected by that group—one male, the other female.

This would be the most prestigious group in town for it would be charged with the community's largest responsibility. It would have a sizable staff, including professional counselors, advisers, placement men and women, and a substantial number of volunteers.

It would be required that every boy and girl register with the local Opportunity Board on reaching age eighteen, or on leaving school before that. There would be a physical check-up provided for, as well as other tests if they weren't available from the schools; followed by a conference with the registrant—routine or considerably more extensive, as circumstance might dictate.

Omitting details (and some difficulties that are obvious), this registration and consultation procedure would be devised to serve two purposes: First, to provide the Human Inventory we need so badly, much more than the rising mountain of faceless statistics that are now accumulating; second, to arrange for every American boy and girl to proceed along the course—education, employment, training, or service—that he or she wants or ought to take.

The responsibility of such a Board would be to make whatever arrangements are necessary, if any are, to provide every individual with the *opportunity*—no more than this, but no less—to go on with his (or her) education, to enter a training program, to go into a service program, or to move into meaningful employment. The Board would have no authority whatsoever to dictate or compel the individual's following one course or another. It would be the individual's agent. There would, however, be insistence that he, or she, *use* the opportunities afforded.

The registration and conference procedure would include a flexible provision for periodic check-ins, check-ups, and check-outs over the next few years.

The proposal, in short, is to do as efficient a job of lining up, registering, young Americans for civilian as for military service, for opportunity as for obligation.

The necessary Point II of such a policy would be to *assure* the *opportunity* to every young American to spend his, or her, critical years in getting ready for what comes after that.

This is less audacious, compared with current accomplishment, than it sounds.

A proper place to start would be with the two-year, eighteen- and nineteen-year-old, age group.

There are today about 6.7 million boys and girls in this age group.

About 3.1 million of this total number are in high school or college. The most reasonable (although rough) estimate is that another 600,000 are in special training, or work-training programs, or are employed as apprentices or trainees in skilled occupations or trades. Some 450,000 are in military service. Another quarter of a million are in other service programs. About 800,000 girls in this age-group are married, and living with their husbands. Another rough estimate is that regardless of what may be done along the suggested lines, as many as one in ten in this group will go directly into what may well prove dead-end jobs.

These figures are only approximations. They indicate, however, that it would be necessary to develop about 750,000 more preparation or job opportunities if a program such as this were to become effective.

This is an achievable program. If the affluent society means anything worth being part of, it means that there *are* these opportunities. But three steps are necessary to improve them.

One is a continued expansion of the educational program even beyond the high levels set by the Eighty-ninth Congress.

The second is a more closely coordinated and integrated, public and private, development of the training and retraining, on-the-job training, vocational rehabilitation and vocational education, Community Action, Neighborhood Youth Corps, Job Corps, and apprenticeship programs.

A third is the development of a broad-scale national service program. This matter, too, is presently before the National Commission on Selective Service, and so I omit any detail—except for strong and unqualified endorsement—and the unnecessary injunction against permitting, in this planning, the military detail to wag the dog.

If this enumeration of necessary implementing steps seems too cavalier, I must necessarily plead the exigencies of time. These will not be easy steps, and they can't be small ones. They will have to depend on social invention more than on increased appropriation, on fuller exploration and development of ideas we have so far only toyed with—or even looked at and set aside:

> The broad expansion, for example, of the cooperative education-work program which Antioch College, Northeastern University and others are proving can bring the costs of education down and its value, for many people, up;

> The repeated proposals (repeatedly, so far, found wanting in some respect) for using tax credits to encourage enlarged employer training programs (as well as increased capital expenditures for equipment);

> The turning of part of the Social Security system around some way so that enough of its benefits (earned during employment) could be drawn on in advance to permit a person to get the training which would be the difference between employment and nonemployment;

> The intriguing idea of a very broad educational or training loan program, with the loan to be repaid by adding a very small percentage to the borrower's income tax rate for a specified number of years; so that he pays on the basis of what the value of the training proves to be (or not to be)— and at the time that value is realized.

Sure we have to invent our future—with all the boldness as citizens that we have as scientists.

It is important to recognize in this connection that the nation's work is going to require a lesser and lesser portion of the hours of people's lives. There is today a substantial movement toward earlier "retirement." This isn't going to make sense—for it comes just when life science is extending people's usefulness and increasing both their ability and their desire to keep on working longer. It would make a good deal more sense to move toward a situation in which it becomes normal to *enter* "employment" two years later—using these years for preparation—instead of leaving it two years earlier —when there is (so far) nothing much else to do.

I have omitted, from this second point, two matters that will present unquestionably hard problems.

One is how to handle the possibility of there being more individuals who want to go to college, or into training programs, or service programs, or into actual jobs, than the available facilities in one or another of these areas permit. Colleges, the administrators of training and service programs, employers, will properly insist on selecting their own entrants.

The present situation, however, is that the limiting factor is not the availability of opportunities so much as it is the inadequate matching of opportunities and the people who need them.

The other omission is of any tie-in here between these various civilian opportunities and the military service obligation.

This is the particular province of the National Commission on Selective Service, and I have tried very hard not to trespass. But two or three points are obviously so essential to the broader development as to come necessarily within the license of this discussion.

No other kind of service or education or employment warrants, in my judgment, exemption from military service *under present circumstances*. But this is at least in part because the present deferment system *adds* the burden of military service on top of the disadvantage of the often inequitable denial of educational (and other) opportunity. It is this *compounding* of inequity which almost compels, as I see it, some kind of lottery system for selection for military service—assuming the continuation of the present differential in educational and other opportunity. If, however, full and equal opportunity were afforded in general, then the worst of this problem would be met; and I think that under those circumstances some better answers than a lottery would emerge to take care of the military service part of it.

The situation would be further improved if voluntary military service were to include—as it does today only incompletely—broad training components that would increase the number of both those who are able, and those who are willing, to perform this service.

I press strongly only the more general point: that whatever decision is reached should not be based on any assumption that some boys are going to be usefully and advantageously occupied and that others are not going to be. The point of the general proposal I am advancing is that they will all be so occupied.

Point III involves the responsibility part of it.

Aversion for any form of compulsion is a deep grain in democracy; and ideally there should be no need for compulsion as part of a program as broad in its promise as the kind suggested here. Any suggestion of compulsion also throws at least the shadow of doubt about constitutionality.

The practical and wisest course would therefore be to see how such a program works on an entirely voluntary basis, and to get some experience before considering a possible *requirement* of participation in it. I would take that course.

There are strong reasons, at the same time, for beginning to think through the possibilities of a firmer, tougher course.

It would be precisely those who present the most serious problems, both for themselves and for the community, who would fail to take advantage of any or all of the options which were offered them; and their continuing derelictions and misdemeanors would make a new system *seem* not to be working even if it were in fact improving the general situation materially.

There is a point at which the community's good sense has to be asserted—as it is now in the case of education up to age sixteen—with respect to someone who has clearly established his lack of any sense, or any sense of responsibility, at all. And that point is not necessarily, or even wisely, *after* he has committed a serious offense.

The compulsory education concept could very sensibly be extended to cover types of training and discipline better suited to the "hard cases"—not as part of the penal system but as part of the educational system, and yet operated on the community's terms, not the boy's.

This will never be an easy decision. But account will properly be taken of the fact that this country is probably more disposed right now to move ahead on the "social welfare" front with sternness than with sympathy. The fact, whether attractive or not, is that concern about juvenile delinquency looms larger today in a good many people's minds than their concern about poverty—even though that may well be the cause of the delinquency.

The sensationalism with which the press plays every instance of youth's "offense"—in terms of illegality as well as dissent—is a gross injustice to the vast majority of young men and women whose standards of conduct and thought probably exceed those they grew up by. The fact remains that the juvenile delinquency rate is today considered this country's most alarming index, and people's fear of walking their own streets at night its worst shame.

The figures showing over 50 per cent of all military draftees being rejected for military service because of their physical or mental condition are not going to be accepted, furthermore, as reflecting a condition which enough of those boys can be expected to straighten out in their own way—even if help is extended to them. We know now from disillusioning experience how few of them will voluntarily accept such help.

There is a cancer here, and the country is ready for surgery.

If it is ready, too, to offer full opportunity, its insistence on commensurate responsibility is not unreasonable.

It is possible today, for the first time in American history, to give every new member of it the opportunity to prepare himself, or herself, for useful lifetime membership. It becomes then a fair bargain that the affording of this opportunity warrants insistence on the obligation to use it.

I have said of a possible "policy for youth" too little to be persuasive, too much to be discreet, hopefully enough to evoke consideration. If I have gone beyond the license of my office, I must draw on the tradition of the university. For this is the place to think and talk things through "while," in Mr. Justice Holmes' putting of it, "there is still doubt, while opposite convictions still keep a battlefront against each other, [while] the time for law has not yet come [because] the notion destined to prevail is not yet entitled to the field."

I have meant to advance only the broad propositions that it is possible now, and time, to develop with respect to the years of transition in people's lives a procedure designed to shape the system of things to the individual's needs—instead of shaping him, too often by inattention, to the needs of the system; and that the next step forward is one in which youth must be willing to match opportunity with responsibility.

A final word: If all I have said seems to you who are here to miss entirely the obvious answer—that all you ask or need is to be left to live your own lives and not to be bothered with any "policy for youth"—then I simply remind you that there is a half of your "generation" that is not represented here tonight. They are what all this is about.

APPENDIX

BIOGRAPHICAL NOTES

BENEZET, LOUIS T. (1915-   ). Born, La Crosse, Wisconsin; A.B., Dartmouth College, 1936; A.M., Reed College, 1939; Ph.D., Columbia University, 1942; many honorary degrees, including LL.D., University of Denver, 1950; University of Pittsburgh, 1953; University of Colorado, 1963; instructor, Hill School, 1936-38; associate in psychology, Reed College, 1938-40; fellow in psychology, City College of New York, 1940-41; associate professor of psychology, Knox College, 1942-43; assistant to chancellor, Syracuse University, 1947-48; president, Allegheny College, 1948-55; president, Colorado College, 1955-63; president, Claremont Graduate School, 1963-   ; educational services officer, USN, 1943-46; trustee, Aspen Institute, 1956-   ; director, American Council on Education, 1961-64; Phi Beta Kappa; author, *General Education in the Progressive College,* 1943.

BROOKE, EDWARD W. (1919-   ). Born, Washington, D.C.; B.S., Howard University, 1940; LL.B., Boston University, 1948; J.D., Portia Law School, Boston, 1963; admitted to Massachusetts bar, 1948; Republican candidate for secretary of state of Massachusetts, 1960; attorney general, Commonwealth of Massachusetts, 1962-66; United States Senate (Republican, Massachusetts), 1967-   ; officer, infantry, World War II; decorated, combat infantry badge; selected as one of the ten outstanding young men, Boston, 1952; member, National Association of Attorneys General; Trial Lawyers Association; Boston Bar Association; received Delta Sigma Rho-Tau Kappa Alpha Speaker of the Year Award, 1967; author, *The Challenge of Change,* 1966. (See also *Current Biography: April 1967.*)

FARBER, SEYMOUR M. (1913-   ). Born, Buffalo, New York; A.B., University of Buffalo, 1931; M.D., Harvard University, 1939; in medical practice, San Francisco, 1946-61; instructor, department of medicine, University of California, San Francisco, 1942-47; assistant professor, 1947-53; associate professor, 1953-61; professor, clinical medicine, 1961-   ; assistant dean for continuing education medicine and health services, 1956-63; dean, 1963-   ; lecturer, University of California School of Public Health, Berkeley, 1948-   ; chief, University of California tuberculosis and chest service, San Francisco General Hospital, 1945-   ; consultant, National Cancer Institute, 1958-60; past president, American College of Chest Physicians; member of many medical societies; author, *Cytological Diagnosis of Lung Cancer*; editor, *The Air We Breathe*, 1961; *Man and Civilization: Conflict and Creativity*, 1963; *Man Under Stress*, 1964; and other publications.

GALLAGHER, WES (1911-   ). Born, San Francisco, California; student, University of San Francisco, 1929, 1931; A.B., Louisiana State University, 1935; reporter, Baton Rouge *State Times*, 1935; Rochester *Democrat and Chronicle*, 1935-36; connected with Associated Press since 1937; foreign correspondent, 1940; chief of military staff for African invasion, 1942; for France, 1944; chief of bureau in Germany, 1945-51; general executive, New York, 1951-54; assistant general manager, 1954-62; general manager, 1962-   ; active in many press associations; named one of outstanding young men in the United States, 1945; author, *Back Door to Berlin*, 1943.

JOHNSON, LYNDON BAINES (1908-   ). Born near Stonewall, Texas; graduate, Johnson City (Texas) high school, 1924; B.S., Southwest State Teachers College, San Marcos, 1930; student, Georgetown University Law School, 1935-36; teacher, public schools, Houston, Texas, 1930-32; secretary to Representative Richard M. Kleberg, 1932-35; state director, National Youth Administration for Texas, 1935-37; member, United States House of Representatives (Democrat, Texas), 1937-49; United States Senate, 1949-61; minority leader, 83rd Congress; majority leader, 84th-86th Congresses; resigned from United States Senate, January 3, 1961; Vice President of the United States, 1961-63; became President of the United States upon the assassination of President Kennedy, November 22, 1963; elected President of the United States, 1964; author, *My Hope for America*, 1964. (See also *Current Biography: 1964*.)

KENNEDY, ROBERT F. (1925-). Born, Brookline, Massachusetts; A.B., Harvard University, 1948; LL.B., Virginia Law School, 1951; honorary degrees, including LL.D., Tufts University, 1958; Fordham University, 1961; admitted to Massachusetts bar, 1951; United States Supreme Court, 1955; attorney, criminal division, Department of Justice, 1951-52; assistant counsel, United States Permanent Subcommittee on Investigations, 1953; assistant counsel, Hoover Commission, 1953; chief counsel, United States Senate Committee on Improper Activities in Labor and Management, 1957-60; Attorney General of the United States, 1961-65; United States Senate (Democrat, New York), 1965- ; served with USNR, 1944-46; named one of ten outstanding young men by United States Junior Chamber of Commerce, 1954; recipient, patriotism award, University of Notre Dame, 1958; author, *The Enemy Within,* 1960; *Just Friends and Brave Enemies,* 1962. (See also *Current Biography: 1958.*)

McGOVERN, GEORGE S. (1922-). Born, Avon, South Dakota; A.B., Dakota Wesleyan University, 1946; A.M., Northwestern University, 1949; Ph.D., 1953; professor of history and political science, Dakota Wesleyan University, 1950-53; executive secretary, Democratic party in South Dakota, 1953-56; United States House of Representatives (Democrat, South Dakota), 1957-61; United States Senate, 1963- ; pilot, USAAF, World War II; recipient, Distinguished Flying Cross; special assistant to the President as director of Food for Peace Program, 1961-62; author, *The Colorado Coal Strike, 1913-1914,* 1953. (See also *Current Biography: March 1967.*)

McNAMARA, ROBERT S. (1916-). Born, San Francisco, California; A.B., University of California, 1937; M.B.A., Harvard University, 1939; honorary degrees, including LL.D., University of California, University of Michigan; assistant professor, business administration, Harvard University, 1940-43; executive, Ford Motor Company, 1946-61; controller, 1949-53; assistant general manager, Ford division, 1953-55; vice president and general manager, 1955-57; president, 1960-61; Secretary of Defense, 1961- ; decorated, Legion of Merit; Phi Beta Kappa. (See also *Current Biography: 1961.*)

READ, DAVID H. C. (1910-   ). Born, Cupar, Fife, Scotland; attended Daniel Stewart's College, Edinburgh; M.A., University of Edinburgh, 1932; B.D., New College, Edinburgh, 1936; became ordained minister, Church of Scotland, 1936; minister, Greenbank Church, Edinburgh, 1939-49; chaplain, University of Edinburgh, 1949-55; chaplain to Her Majesty the Queen, Scotland, 1952-56; minister, Madison Avenue Presbyterian Church, 1956-   ; author, *The Spirit of Life,* 1939; *Prisoner's Quest,* 1944; *I Am Persuaded,* 1962; and other publications.

REISCHAUER, EDWIN O. (1910-   ). Born, Tokyo, Japan; graduate of American school, Tokyo, 1927; A.B., Oberlin College, 1931; A.M., Harvard University, 1932; Ph.D., 1939; D.Litt., Oberlin College, 1957; instructor, Harvard University, 1938-42; associate professor of Far Eastern Languages, Harvard University, 1946-50; professor, 1950-61; chairman, Japan-Korea Secretariat, special assistant to director, Office of Far Eastern Affairs, Department of State, 1945-46; United States Ambassador to Japan, 1961-66; professor, Harvard University, 1966-   ; with United States Military Intelligence Service, 1943-44; awarded Legion of Merit; president, Far Eastern Association, 1955-56; Phi Beta Kappa; co-author, *Translations from Early Japanese Literature,* 1951; *East Asia, The Great Tradition,* 1960; author, *Japan, Past and Present,* 1946; *Wanted: An Asian Policy,* 1955; *The United States and Japan,* 1957; and other publications. (See also *Current Biography: 1962.*)

WIRTZ, WILLIAM WILLARD (1912-   ). Born, De Kalb, Illinois; attended Northern Illinois State Teachers College, De Kalb, 1928-30; University of California, Berkeley, 1930-31; A.B., Beloit College, 1933; LL.B., Harvard University Law School, 1937; instructor, Kewaunee (Illinois) high school, 1933-34; instructor of law, State University of Iowa, 1937-39; assistant professor of law, Northwestern University, 1939-42; professor of law, 1946-54; assistant general counsel, Board of Economic Warfare, 1942-43; general counsel, War Labor Board, 1945; chairman, National Wage Stabilization Board, 1946; in private law practice, 1955-61; associated professionally and politically with Adlai E. Stevenson; Secretary of Labor, 1962-   ;

Phi Beta Kappa; Delta Sigma Rho. (See also *Current Biography:
1963.*)

YOUNG, WHITNEY M., JR. (1921-   ). Born, Lincoln Ridge, Kentucky; B.S., Kentucky State College, 1941; student, Massachusetts Institute of Technology, 1942-43; A.M., University of Minnesota, 1947; student, Harvard University, 1960-61; industrial relations and vocational guidance director, St. Paul Urban League, 1947-50; executive secretary, Omaha Urban League, 1950-53; dean, School of Social Work, Atlanta University, 1954-60; executive director, National Urban League, 1961-   ; member, advisory board, New York School of Social Work; national advisory council, AFL-CIO community services committee; served with AUS, World War II; recipient, Florina Lasker award, 1959; outstanding alumni award, University of Minnesota, 1960; author, *Status of the Negro Community,* 1959; *Integration: The Role of Labor Education,* 1959; *Intergroup Relations as a Challenge to Social Work Practice,* 1960; co-author, *A Second Look: The Negro Citizen in Atlanta,* 1958. (See also *Current Biography: 1965.*)

CUMULATIVE AUTHOR INDEX

1960-1961—1966-1967

A cumulative author index to the volumes of REPRESENTATIVE AMERICAN SPEECHES for the years 1937-1938 through 1959-1960 appears in the 1959-1960 volume.